Tottenham 'Til I Die

Published by
Legends Publishing
18 Darby Crescent
Sunbury-on-Thames
Middlesex
TW16 5LA

Tel 01932 783314
E-mail david@legendspublishing.net
Web www.tilidie.co.uk or www.legendspublishing.net

Introduction

I am delighted that Tottenham Hotspur Foundation has produced this wonderful collection of fans' stories. Tottenham 'Til I Die is much more than nostalgia, it is a fascinating social history seen through the eyes of Spurs fans from seven to 92 and from all corners of the world. Reading the book one cannot help but be overwhelmed by the power our Club has to inspire loyalty and passion and it is this same passion that we harness in the Foundation's work. Using football to engage and inspire, the Foundation last year offered over 500,000 sporting opportunities to young people and local communities across North London – creating opportunities that really can change lives. All proceeds from the sale of this book will be used to fund further Tottenham Hotspur Foundation literacy projects.

Tottenham 'Til I Die is as much about the process of writing as the book itself; preparation took the team into schools, brought groups of senior citizens in to work in the Club's Learning Zone and has seen best-selling children's author and fanatical Spurs fan, Darren Shan, thrilling over 150 local school children with tales of following the Club. We are honoured that Darren has contributed his own exclusive story to this book as a foreword.

Tottenham Hotspur Football Club has a glittering history captured in these pages and now with the new stadium being planned and the training ground in development we are at the start of an exciting new chapter in the life of our Club. New fans and new stories are created every day and we look forward to you all being part of our future. Come on you Spurs!

Daniel Levy

Foreword

I'm a Spurs fan because of my uncle Derek, and he's a fan because of my mum, but really it was all the fault of an Easter egg! Derek's only a few years older than me. When he was three, my mum bought him an Easter egg that came in a Spurs mug. He liked the mug, so he took an interest in the team, and that's how the legacy began. One of my earliest memories is of a match played in September 1978. We lost 7-0 to Liverpool – ouch! I didn't know much about football back then, and I had some photos of Liverpool players stuck up on my bedroom wall. Derek made me take them down and rip them up into tiny pieces. I got off lucky that day. A friend of mine called Kevin was a Liverpool fan, but after that shocker of a result, his older brother Jimmy made him convert to Spurs. To sever all links, Jimmy told Kevin to hold out his beloved Liverpool scarf, then he set it on fire! It can be a dangerous business, being a fan!!!

I loved supporting Spurs in the early 1980s. It was the era of Ossie, Ricky and Glenn. We won the FA Cup two years in a row and I watched the finals on the TV, which was a rare treat in those days. Very few games were shown live, especially in Ireland where I lived. In fact the 1984 UEFA Cup Final wasn't shown on TV in Ireland! I had to listen to it on a radio in my bedroom. The signal kept fading, so I had to keep moving the radio around. In the end that didn't matter. Not being able to see anything when it went to a penalty shoot-out made it even more thrilling!

That was one of my proudest moments as a Spurs fan. Winning in England is a joy, but being able to say you support the best team in a European competition was extra special. It's been 25 years since we were last able to make such a boast, but our day will come again, I'm sure it will.

The match I probably most enjoyed was the 1991 FA Cup semi-final. We were massive underdogs in that game. Arsenal were by far the best team in England. They played horrible, boring football, but they were just about impossible to beat. Until a certain Paul Gascoigne stepped up and struck a wonder goal! I was watching the game in my grandparents' house in London. I jumped around the room, screaming my head off with delight. My Granny came running — she thought something was wrong! I don't remember most of that game, but those few seconds are etched into my mind for life. That's what football's all about — the glory of the moment. We endure a lot as fans, games that seem to last an age, losses, disappointments, setbacks. And it's the same for fans everywhere.

But those moments of magic keep us going. Ricky jinking his way through the ranks of Man City... Gazza putting Arsenal to the sword... Ginola's wonder season where he could do no wrong... scoring five goals against the Arsenal... Woodgate heading in the winner to deny Chelsea the Carling Cup on our first return to the new Wembley. We're lucky, as Spurs fans, to have a whole host of great memories. Even though the last 20 years haven't been our most glorious, we've seen some amazing players grace the turf at White Hart Lane — Lineker, Klinsmann, Davids, Berbatov, Robbie Keane and more. There have been Cup Finals, famous victories, a sustained presence in Europe.

This book collects the memories of a whole host of Spurs fans, and I can't wait to read them. Each fan has their own store of highlights. By sharing these stories, we can all be reminded of games we'd forgotten, incidents we hadn't thought about for ages, players who had slipped our minds. Football isn't just about matches - it's about sharing recollections of those games with your friends. One of the things I love best about going to The Lane (I've been a season ticket holder for eight years now and make most of our home games, even though I still live in Ireland!) is meeting up with my friends, chatting about past games and players, coming up with lists like our five favourite goals, the worst forward to ever wear the shirt, the best left winger we've ever had.

This book isn't just a record of stories. It's a way to generate debate, to get us remembering and talking. I plan to scour this book from first page to last, to be reminded of great conquests, terrible losses, nights of pleasure and days we'd rather forget. It's not often that we get a chance to share our experiences like this, so it's an opportunity we should all seize happily and make the most of. I'm especially interested to find out if anybody else became a Spurs fan because of an Easter egg!

Darren Shan © 2009

As an Edinburgh born and bred Spurs fan I may not make it to many games, but my passion for the Lilywhites is no less than that of fans who visit The Lane every other weekend. I have supported Spurs pretty much my entire life and I can still remember them being the first team I 'really' watched on TV and taking an instant shine to a club that would bring me so much joy, disappointment and frustration, plus many a thick ear in the playground from fellow pupils who supported teams north of the border and didn't take kindly to my N17 allegiances. Then there were the kick-abouts in the playground.

While friends pretended they were Kenny Dalglish, Graeme Souness or Andy Gray, I was always Glenn Hoddle. Needless to say I bore the brunt of the hefty challenges, some of which resulted in bloody noses, black eyes or, more often, the most passionate of arguments with kids who were mostly Hearts supporters. But it was at primary school where I pulled off one of my most crafty Spurs moments and one of the most visible demonstrations of how much the club meant to me.

One day I conveniently 'forgot' to let my mum know that it was photograph day and turned up, not in school shirt and tie or best clothes like most of the other kids in my class, but in my freshly washed and ironed Spurs top! I remember standing tall and pushed out my chest while dreaming of one day running out at White Hart Lane. I wouldn't part with this photo for the world, but I still remember mum was none too impressed when I took it home and the incident was mentioned at the next parents-teacher evening! Today, my life is no less eventful.

After unwittingly being set up on a blind date by a mate, I met my darling wife. Unfortunately, she and all her clan are Gooners, which makes family get-togethers tense sometimes, but it's not all bad. Gracie, my young daughter, has started to show an allegiance to Tottenham, something I'll do all I can to encourage. However, I can assure you that she will not be wearing a Spurs shirt on class photo day – not because I wouldn't let her – but because her Gooner mum would kill us both!

Justin Hynd

RISKING EVERYTHING FOR TOTTENHAM

In 1961 I had pursued my education in England where I saw Tottenham on television. I was completely captivated by the club and my passion has grown over the years despite the frustrations. However, it was another captivation that affected my life even more dramatically.

It seems that Third World countries all too easily dive into needless conflicts and it was during the Iraq-Iran war that I was held in captivity for 3,080 days. My grief was made worse due to total ignorance of how Tottenham were getting on. No radios were permissible and violators would risk life threatening punitive measures including 60 lashes. I took the risk and it was in 1984-85, almost three years after falling captive, when I was at last able to acquire some Spurs news. If I had been caught my punishment would have been vicious, as other prisoners with radios found to their cost.

After seven years of captivity, I decided to give up smoking and I was able to trade my tobacco savings for a gold necklace and a ring from other prisoners. These were given to an Iranian soldier with an appetite for gold items. He was good and brought the radio set, which

[Right] Emad now enjoying a safer life in Qatar

he concealed inside a packet of salt. One prisoner, who had been a professional mason before the war, was used extensively by the authorities for construction work at the Iranian quarters inside the camp. Upon his daily return he was always allowed to make a stopover at the Iranian canteen to buy whatever he could afford as a reward for his contributions. On that day, he was told to take the packet of salt inside the camp without knowing of its real contents and to hand it over to a certain prisoner. That he did without any notice, particularly from the prisoners' side.

The radio set was smaller than the palm of my hand; a black *Lucky* brand made in Hong Kong with two extra small batteries and an ear set. I impatiently waited for eight o'clock when the night curfew always started and all prisoners were inside their respective tents. Only then could I possibly put the radio on and listen to my favourite stations using the earphones, while covering my head with my two blankets in the freezing cold weather conditions. Even my tent-mates, with whom there was full trust, had no knowledge of what was going on. At the same time my plans would allow only 30 minutes use of the radio per night, twice a week, for battery conservation.

But on that night it was the first time in more than two years since I had listened to a BBC news bulletin and I was not surprised that nothing drastic had changed in terms of content or presentation – the fact that nothing in the nine-minute bulletin mentioned the Iraq-Iran war did not surprise me either. However, I felt overwhelmed listening to news linking me with the outside world. I felt, at least momentarily, as if I was part of the civilised world; 'living' like a human being.

Listening to English football commentary for a few minutes, due to the limitations of the situation, was the icing on the cake – regardless of the fact it did not involve Tottenham. However, I was now able to listen to the football results and realised, at last, why the Swiss International Red Cross delegate could not, despite my persistent questions on their visits, tell me anything about Tottenham news even though he was more conversant on Manchester United. Tottenham were still not the team they once were under the late Bill Nicholson in the early 60s and specific news was non-existent it seemed.

After repatriation to Iraq in 1990, I found bans imposed on satellite TV, with prison terms and hefty fines threatened. The Iraqi regime had imposed a penalty of US$400, which was then the equivalent of an annual salary or even more for a mid-level government employee. In addition, there was a prison term of six months and the satellite receiver and dish would be confiscated. But again, I paid no attention.

After 2003 I was at last able to watch all games without fear, or this was what I had thought. I will always remember a very memorable goal scored by Frederic Kanoute against Everton at the Lane. It could not have been more well timed because, just as the ball crossed the line, there was a huge spontaneous explosion near my home which blew a thick wooden door at the front of my house right to the back of the property.

Today, I am a grandfather. One of my sons is a Tottenham fan and I am sure one of my grandsons will follow suit. To me Tottenham remind me of my youth and I feel very much attached to the club. My deep memory takes me back to the time when White Hart Lane was a fortress no other team could conquer. Although I have never been to White Hart Lane, and attending a home game is still a far-fetched life's ambition, both my son and I buy t-shirts, caps, publications and other items for the kids annually. It is the least support we can provide for the club we are so much devoted to.

Emad Nimah

Meet Banner Boy

My name is Dylan and I am nine years old. I live in London Colney and come to White Hart Lane with my mum. To many Tottenham Hotspur supporters I am known as 'Banner Boy', in fact you may have seen me in the North Stand as I take a banner to nearly every home game. The fans around always ask me what the banner will be for the next match, but I always keep it as a surprise.

I make the banners at home with my mum, they take about three hours, so I try to get them signed by the players if I can. After the match my mum frames them for me and they are all on my bedroom walls. My friends think what I

do is really great, some of them even saw me on TV with my Defoe banner at the Burnley match. My favourite is probably 'Merry Christmas Harry's Hotspurs' as it has all of the players pictured on it. I think my 'Reliant Robbie' banner was good too. When Robbie Keane left I was really upset, he was my favourite player and I tried my hardest to play football like him, so the 'Bentley versus Keane' banner was funny. I was very pleased when he returned to Spurs!

I really enjoy going to the games and cheering on the players, it is such a great atmosphere at White Hart Lane. I was a mascot back in November and I came out with Aaron Lennon, it was a great experience and Lennon was man of the match that day too!

Spurs has always been in my family, my grandad used to take my mum, Kelly, to games when she was little and my uncle Ricky sits in the South Stand with his girlfriend and my other uncle, Scott, has a season ticket too. I will definitely be Tottenham 'til I die!

Dylan Rushton *with a selection of his fantastic banners*

Gilly To The Rescue

I have always had a thing about autographs, particularly those of my beloved Spurs players. This started when I was a young kid, and developed further during my teens. In the late 60s and 70s, before every Spurs game outside of London, I would meet the first team players at the station and 'travel' with them on the train, which was the normal mode of transport in those days for footballers. For games in the north, the team would go up on a Friday and I would travel back with them. For nearer games, the team would go on Saturday morning and I would be on the train there and back.

The players got to know me because they saw me on every trip. My speciality was to secure card tables for the team to use in the first class carriages. They were like gold dust, but I had a knack of getting them by raiding every other train in the station! In return, the deal was that the players would sign all my photos and I would get a ticket for the match. They were real legends in those days: Jennings, Knowles, Kinnear, Mullery, England, Gilzean, Greaves and Chivers. They were true Spurs heroes – how I miss that team. Without complaint they all signed no end of photos, a collection I still have to this day.

But disaster struck one weekend, before an away trip to Derby... when I reached St. Pancras station I realised I had left most of my money at home. Despite this devastating error, I put my personal disappointment to one side and dutifully organised the card tables as normal and greeted the players aboard, before I alighted and started to walk sadly back down the platform towards the exit, then back home instead of on to the Baseball Ground.

Two more of Martin's treasured photo collection [above] Phil Beal and [left] Martin Chivers

Previous page photos are of Alan Gilzean and Jimmy Greaves

"Hey! What's up?" Gilly shouted out of the window. I told him I had left my money at home. Then, without a second's hesitation, he pulled out a crisp £20 note, which was a lot of money in those days, and suggested I should give it back to him on the next trip – away to Southampton. He went on to tell me that I was to meet him outside the ground in Derby, where he would give me a ticket. I sat behind Alf Ramsey in the Directors' Box that day!

As agreed, I took the replacement £20 to the Southampton match and, as soon as I saw Gilly at the station, offered to repay him. However, the player insisted that I keep the money, "As a present for Christmas", which was only a week away. Can you imagine that happening these days, let alone being able to get so close and friendly with such a great player? I will always remember that great gesture and wonder how many modern day stars would be that generous to a lad who, in reality, was probably a bit of a pest. But they recognised true supporters as part of the scene.

I'm an accountant now and proud to say that some of those Spurs legends are my clients. Joe Kinnear and Paul Miller can't believe that I am the same kid from the trains and I also know Pat Jennings and Steve Perryman. Pat recently re-introduced me to Philip Beal, who was my favourite player from those days. We shook hands and I asked him if he knew who I was? He took one look at me and, to my complete amazement said, "You used to travel with us didn't you?" That really made my day! It's nearly 40 years ago and he still remembered me. We both had a good laugh and a good reminisce.

Martin Taylor

Memorable Cup Run

TOTTENHAM HOTSPUR N⁰ 4378
Football & Athletic Co. Ltd.

U.E.F.A. CUP FINAL
(2nd leg)
TOTTENHAM HOTSPUR
v
WOLVERHAMPTON WANDERERS
On Wednesday, 17th May, 1972
(or date when played, see National Press)
Kick-off 7.45 p.m.

50p GROUND
TICKET

The Tottenham Hotspur
Company do not Guarantee
that the proposed match will
be played.
G. W. JONES
Secretary

THIS PORTION TO BE RETAINED

In the event of a postponement this ticket will be valid for the rearranged date.
Thomas Knight & Co. Ltd., The Clock House Press, Hoddesdon, Herts.

I will never forget the day we won the UEFA Cup at White Hart Lane by beating Wolverhampton Wanderers. I was beside myself with excitement, it was my first Cup Final and as the big match approached I could think of nothing else. There was a crowd of us going, my uncle had arranged to take me and we agreed he would meet me at the bottom of my road.

As you can imagine, I was there in good time, kitted out and ready to go. And there I stood. I waited and waited and waited, until way past our agreed meet time. I was frantic; I knew I would already be missing the exciting build up to kick off. Where was he?!? What had happened to him?

Suddenly it dawned on me, the answer was simple, in all the excitement my uncle had actually forgotten to pick me up. But there was absolutely no way I was going to miss that final and desperate times call for desperate measures. With no time to hang around any further or waste any more precious time waiting for a bus, I chose the 'route one' solution and decided to run all the way to the ground – all the way from Chingford.

Although I had always been a good runner, it was at sprinting and what faced me now was a marathon. As I passed the Cooks Ferry pub I paused and thought how nice a drink would be, but I had to press on, as a quick glance at my watch showed that the players would soon be coming out.

Although by that stage my legs were saying 'no more', the adrenalin and the threat of missing Tottenham's opening goal 'spurred' me on all the way to The Lane. Believe me, despite virtual exhaustion, the relief at finally reaching the stadium was immense.

The match had already started by the time I impatiently clicked my way through the turnstiles and the ground was of course heaving and, because I'm not exactly the tallest of people, I remember spending most of the firsthalf weaving between spectators trying to catch a glimpse of the game. Although I was never going to get the view I was hoping for, just being there was all that mattered to me. The only clear view I really wanted to see was thankfully granted to me; the Spurs players parading the cup around The Lane!

Despite aching legs for a few days afterwards, everything had been worthwhile; I was there to see history being made. Needless to say my uncle John could not apologise enough and was off my Christmas card list for quite a while.

Martin Brown

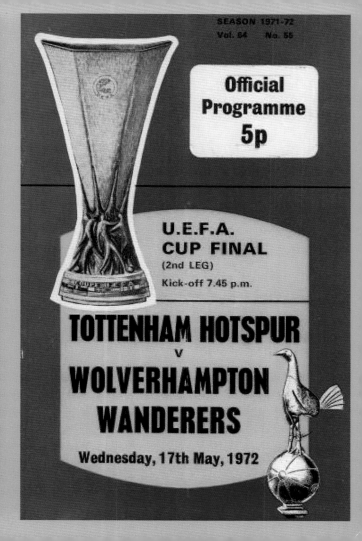

SEASON 1971-72
Vol. 64   No. 55

Official
Programme
5p

U.E.F.A.
CUP FINAL
(2nd LEG)
Kick-off 7.45 p.m.

TOTTENHAM HOTSPUR
v
WOLVERHAMPTON
WANDERERS

Wednesday, 17th May, 1972

Scooting To The Lane

It was 1 December 1962, Spurs versus Everton, 0-0. Spurs went on to win the European Cup-Winners Cup that season but Everton went on to win the First Division title. Greaves was top scorer over Everton's Vernon. I travelled all the way to White Hart Lane from Brownswood Road, near Clissold Park, on my push scooter. I would go up Green Lanes, past the castellated water works to Manor House and then along the Seven Sisters Road.

I met a mate called Christopher who had brought along our prized model chicken, which we had 'borrowed' from a Courage Pub and painted with thick white gloss!! I had a knack of resting its beak on the handle bar of my scooter and holding it against the bar with one knee. I would have lots of plastic star badges pinned to my jumper featuring favourites like Peter Baker, John White and Terry Medwin, a floppy rosette with Bobby Smith's face smiling out like one of the garden friends of Bill & Ben the flower pot men.

When we got to the stadium we just left our scooters by a wall and there was never a thought that anyone would nick them, but then I also remember nobody ever had bicycle chains back then. Maybe they were more honest times? My dad had given me a florin (two shillings) instead of my usual Saturday present of an Airfix airplane model, and I had been saving for a couple of weeks by NOT getting *The Beezer* comic so that I could make up the money in case I had to get a bus or buy a hot Bovril.

When we arrived it was actually hard to get near to a turnstile because of the volume of people. But as we were little, we would dodge in and out and the men wouldn't mind letting us lads in before them.

I think about 60,000 went in on that freezing Saturday afternoon. And before the final whistle it became even colder as the light faded. Nearly all of the men smoked then and you could see the clouds rising from the mass of standing spectators in the floodlights. We used to go and stand by the rosette and badge men and study the ground around where they were selling intently and often would find a 3d bit or, if we were lucky, a 6d piece.

If we needed the odd sixpence to make up our ticket price we would just go up and ask men to "lend us" a tanner (6d). In those days there were 'pirate' programme sellers, trying to con away fans and on that day I picked one such programme up from the gutter obviously thrown away in disgust when the buyer realised he had been duped. These were not forerunners of the fanzines, which came in the late 80s, but fake programmes no doubt printed by unscrupulous printers.

The return journey after the game was easier because it was downhill from Manor House, but when I got home, and I'll never forget this, I couldn't take my socks off because they had frozen to my feet! But what did I care? I had that sense of having been part of the very centre of football and that feeling has lasted for nearly fifty years. Part of the excitement was being able to tell Mr. Smith, my head teacher at Ambler Road Primary, all about it on the Monday, although he was an Arsenal supporter.

Nowadays it is almost unthinkable that parents would allow a 10-year-old to travel alone on a push scooter, on a freezing winter's day, such a long way to see a football match that drew such a vast crowd, then to come home alone in the dark. But I was there at White Hart Lane amongst dozens of similar boys who had all come to the game alone. I can't help thinking just how lucky I was to have been young in those glory days, star-struck and dreaming of my heroes. For the price of an Airfix model and a couple of *Beezer*'s I could actually go and see the greatest team there ever was.

Steve Cowan *pictured at home on his bike*

Tattooed Hotspur

My love affair with Tottenham Hotspur began on 10 August 1968; it was the day that my mum took me as a nine-year-old to see the team my father and grandfather both supported.

I remember taking the bus from Wood Green and the walk towards the High Road when we alighted – the noise of the crowd, the hustle and bustle of match day, the assorted vendors, hot chestnuts on a brazier, the burger trolleys, the Percy Dalton man with his bags of peanuts in their shells and the rosette man with his call, "Get yer team colours".

My mum bought me a navy blue and white ribboned rosette with a small foil effigy of the FA Cup in the centre and,

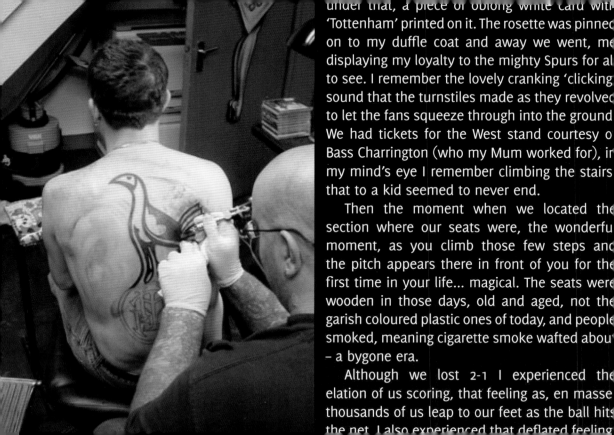

under that, a piece of oblong white card with 'Tottenham' printed on it. The rosette was pinned on to my duffle coat and away we went, me displaying my loyalty to the mighty Spurs for all to see. I remember the lovely cranking 'clicking' sound that the turnstiles made as they revolved to let the fans squeeze through into the ground. We had tickets for the West stand courtesy of Bass Charrington (who my Mum worked for), in my mind's eye I remember climbing the stairs that to a kid seemed to never end.

Then the moment when we located the section where our seats were, the wonderful moment, as you climb those few steps and the pitch appears there in front of you for the first time in your life... magical. The seats were wooden in those days, old and aged, not the garish coloured plastic ones of today, and people smoked, meaning cigarette smoke wafted about – a bygone era.

Although we lost 2-1 I experienced the elation of us scoring, that feeling as, en masse thousands of us leap to our feet as the ball hits the net. I also experienced that deflated feeling

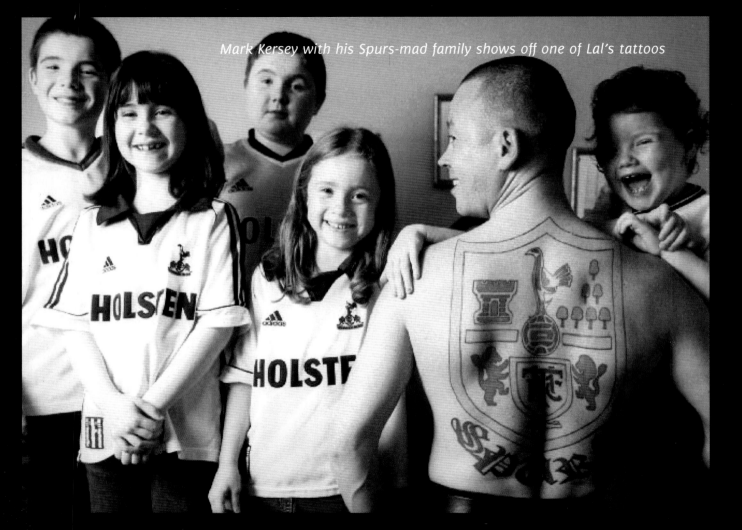

Mark Kersey with his Spurs-mad family shows off one of Lal's tattoos

twice, as the opposition hit our net. But no matter the result, I was hooked, bitten by the Tottenham bug, never to recover. Tottenham 'til I die!

In 1978, I embarked on my career as a tattoo artist. Few people got football tattoos in those days, and those that did lived up to the strereotype and were either working class lads or yobs, or both. And just like in football, how times have changed over the years – I have embellished the flesh of literally hundreds and hundreds of Spurs fans with tattoos devoted to Tottenham Hotspur. Nowadays the tattoo trade knows no bounds, customers of both sexes and of all classes, creeds and colours proudly wear the colours of THFC .

A couple of years ago Lady Luck dealt me a fantastic hand when I was called upon to tattoo Darren Bent, Robbie Keane, Dimitar Berbatov, Jermain Defoe, Ledley King, Aaron Lennon, Tom Huddlestone, Jamie O'Hara, Vedran Corluka, Kevin Prince Boateng, plus many young Spurs were also visitors to the studio. During their visits I was able to talk at length with players about all things Tottenham and hear from the players who were in the victorious Carling Cup final against Chelsea. We talked about the elation and jubilation of winning silverware and what it feels like to play at Wembley, how it was to see a sea of blue and white flags and what the noise was like from the pitch. I was also privileged to speak about many things concerning the club with some of our great players that would have been nice to share in this book, but the conversations took place within the privacy of the studio and, out of respect, that is where they shall have to remain.

Lal Hardy *pictured above with Aaron Lennon*

SPURS FOREVER

In many ways I count myself lucky to have gone to games at the end of the Second World War, even though Spurs were in the old Second Division. In those days a lot of the players lived locally and we would see them going into training on our way to school. Most of the training was carried out at the stadium – the club didn't move to Cheshunt for training purposes until 1952. Sometimes the players would train on the St. Ignatius College sports fields, situated at the back of the East Stand, and us boys would often watch them going through their paces and then collect autographs, an activity which really came into its own during the school holidays.

Most of the players used to arrive for training by bus or on foot, only a small handful owned a car back then, and that is where we'd corner them for their signatures. At times, believe it or not, we would even go round to players' houses for autographs – several lived very near to me in the eastern side of Enfield. Once, I knocked on the door of Horace Woodward [pictured above], who had joined Tottenham in March 1939, played during the War, then made his Football League debut, replacing the unavailable Bill Nicholson, in a 4-2 victory over Newport County. As she opened the door, Horace's wife called out to inform her husband that a little boy had knocked wanting his autograph, but as he emerged from the sitting room, I remember him saying, "Oh, not you again, you nuisance!" Collecting autographs was great fun though, and us lads regarded most of the players as our friends and, so soon after the War, this entertainment was great!

Among my early match-day memories are FA Cup ties at home to West Bromwich Albion and Leicester City, with both attendances around the 70,000 mark. The huge crowds meant that a lot of us boys had to sit on the touchline and, to our credit, we did not invade the pitch when Tottenham scored. Cup matches were so popular back in those days and I will always remember being locked out of White Hart Lane in 1952 when Cup holders, Newcastle United, were the opponents and there was another colossal attendance. The excitement of winning promotion with the 'push and run' team in 1950 will also always live in the memory, followed by taking the First Division by storm and finishing Champions of the land.

In those days football was still often played on Christmas Day mornings and two such matches stand out clearly more than half a century later; a 7-1 win against Middlesbrough in 1952, and a 6-0 drubbing of Everton in 1956. Even the reserve team would play games on December 25th, which I also went to see, in what was clearly a very different era.

Reserve games were great fun, and I was fortunate to be present to witness the excitement when the reserves recorded a 13-0 mauling of Brighton in August 1947, Len Duquemin scored a hatful that day, before going on to become a first team regular over the next decade.

Dave Mackay

By 1954 I was going to quite a few away games, often visiting our hosts' supporters clubs up north in the evening after the match. Visits to Aston Villa, Burnley, Bolton and Hull were always very enjoyable in that respect. Only recently I went to Spurs' game at Hull's new stadium and was surprised to read a feature in their match-day programme, which mentioned a tour of the fish docks that was arranged for both sets of supporters in 1954 that I went on! The day I got demobbed from the RAF, Spurs had a home game and beat Birmingham City 7-1, I remember thinking what a wonderful 'welcome home' present that was for me. Alf Stokes scored five that day!

The arrival of Dave Mackay in March 1959 saw a great upturn in Tottenham's fortunes, and the wonderful Double side was taking shape. As Spurs had never played at Wembley before 1961, the excitement and anticipation of that Cup Final was a feeling no fan lucky enough to be there will ever forget. During that Cup run I was at Roker Park for the Sixth Round clash with Sunderland when Spurs fans made an exodus from London to cheer the players on to a well-earned 1-1 draw. A superb 5-0 win in the replay back on home turf saw off the Wearsiders in front of another capacity crowd.

I also count myself extremely lucky to have been in Rotterdam during May 1963 when we beat Atletico Madrid 5-1 to win the European Cup Winners' Cup – one of Spurs' finest hours. The next day victorious supporters made celebratory excursions to see the famous Dutch bulb fields and the canals – everybody had such a wonderful couple of days and we were made to feel so welcome. What a contrast to the events of 1974.

Like all experienced Tottenham fans I have so many happy memories of following this great club and, even though they are mixed with a fair share of disappointments – amazingly home defeats to the likes of Chesterfield and Lincoln back in the 1940s still spring to mind – I wish I could carry on coming to watch Spurs forever.

Chris Stevens *[pictured] Danny Blanchflower before the memorable win over Atletico Madrid*

Our Love Is King

It was 1962 and I was seven-years-old – it was my first game. Three generations of male "Kings" stood side by side on the packed terraces. My father and grandfather either side of me, helping me to balance, as I stood on an upturned milk crate, which still left me short of seeing all the action. I don't remember the game, just the atmosphere... and Jimmy Greaves.

I had heard tales throughout my short life of the "Spurs", tales of passion and wondrous skills. I had heard anecdotes of the previous year, when the wonderful Double was accomplished, and the elder two Kings had gone to two Wembley Cup Finals. The local amateur team, Walthamstow Avenue, won the Amateur Cup. And yes they went with the wrong tickets but still got in somehow. They told me a story of how the band had played *John Brown's Body* and it was they who had started the crowd singing "and the Spurs go marchin' on".

At that first game my life changed there and then, not just because of family tradition, but because I knew living would be incomplete without the passion and tears that this game and the Lilywhites were to bring me. Since then I have been to every semi and final since 1971, including Feyenoord, and 95% of all home games, standing at the Park Lane, or now, sitting in the East Stand. I've seen the artistry of Ardiles, Gilzean, Gascoigne, Conn, Ginola, Hoddle, yes and Berbatov. I've felt the passion of Perryman, Roberts, Mackay, Mabbutt, King, Knowles, Beal and Gough. In recent years my life has flashed before me, both at the 125th Anniversary game and with the passing of Bill Nicholson. Unannounced tears were shed just from pure emotion. For this part of my life I am truly grateful. Thank you Spurs – Glory Glory!

Dave King *pictured with his old, home made Spurs rattle*

The Right Priorities

It was the morning of 8 January 1977. The winter was particularly harsh that year and, with Spurs at the bottom of the League, a trip to Second Division Cardiff in the FA Cup seemed like light relief. My 15-year-old car was always going to be pushed to its limits and, with only 10 miles to go, the poor over-heated engine gave up the ghost and spluttered to its death as if choking on a renegade peanut.

As we stood and paid our last respects to the car an elderly gent was passing in his shiny new one, so, in an act of desperation, we beckoned him to stop. Thankfully, he willingly agreed. By this stage, the time was rapidly approaching 2.30pm and, when he heard of our dilemma, the man kindly offered us a lift straight to the ground. We arrived at exactly 2.59pm. We thanked our saviour kindly, then bolted through the first turnstile we saw, frantic not to miss the start of the match. Running up the stairs to the terraces we could hear the roar as the whistle blew to start the game. Now, at this point, you may think this story has a happy ending, but alas, we had been deposited at Cardiff's rugby ground. In a scene reminiscent of a 70's *Carry On* film, we ran back down the steps and, after explaining why we must get out, found ourselves desperately looking for a cab outside the rugby stadium. We did eventually get to Ninian Park, only to see the boys lose 1-0 and were forced to come back to London on a supporters' coach. As an epitaph, I was later charged by the police with 'abandonment of a vehicle' and fined £20. But perhaps our FA Cup mishap in South Wales shouldn't have come as a complete surprise in the first place.

The previous season Spurs had been held at home to Stoke in the Cup and, urged on by the lads, the replay seemed like a good idea when it was mentioned. My friend had just installed a new

8-track stereo in his Ford Corsair and, with the volume blaring, we drove the 150 miles north to the Victoria Ground. Now, had we had the radio on, we would have heard that strong gusts of wind had blown away part of the roof of City's main stand, meaning the game had been called off for safety reasons, while we were rocking our way north. Under normal circumstances you would just turn round and drive home again and just accept what had happened as unfortunate, but not the end of the world. This, however, was no 'ordinary' evening. With my Spurs blinkers on I had totally forgotten that I was due to meet my fiancée that night to confirm the purchase of a house ahead of our imminent wedding. While she stood shivering, waiting for me outside Romford Station, I was somewhere in the East Midlands looking for a half-decent restaurant to stuff my face. Well, after some delicate negotiation and no end of apologies, I can tell you that the wedding did take place as planned, however, you can probably guess that it ended in divorce shortly afterwards.

Harvey Harris *pictured above on his wedding day!*

Ten Bob Transfer Fee

My dad was a Spurs fans, as was his dad, in fact my grandad did some of the building work on the original East Stand and ever since then the family has followed Spurs even though we all come from E17. But I am ashamed to say that I almost chose a claret and blue path in life, but thankfully, in 1969, when I was nine years old, my soul was saved! I remember I was playing with a kid over the road, who was a couple of years younger than me, but who was not really interested in football. His dad was a mad Hammers fan and decided to give me a framed photo of Bobby Moore, Geoff Hurst and Martin Peters, plus a West Ham rosette. I remember this happened on a Monday evening and I proudly went home and declared to my dad that I was West Ham.

Even though there was no fuss from my dad at that precise moment, he obviously was hurt by this, because the next day he said I was going to the dentist and, if I was a good boy, there would be a treat coming to me. After a well behaved trip to have my teeth checked, I found

*[Above] Gary and his mates on
The Shelf back in 1978*

*[Left] Cup Final day 1982, Gary
[far left] with his brother, Dave
and mate, Dicky Ledwin*

myself at White Hart Lane for a Spurs versus Ipswich match under the floodlights, a 2-2 draw in which Peter Collins scored. And then it happened.

As I stood on the Shelf with my West Ham rosette pinned to my coat, this old man, who was a complete stranger, came up to us and asked me about the rosette. He said to me, "If I give you a ten bob note (10 shillings) and my scarf and rosette will you support Spurs instead?" Needless to say we swapped. I then watched on as he unravelled the Hammers' rosette and tossed it away like an old fag butt. I have been Spurs mad since, and have even taught my own kids to support Spurs before they could walk and took each one to White Hart Lane before they were five years of age to make sure history didn't repeat itself!

Although ten shillings bought me, nobody could question that I have blue and white blood running through my veins these days – something I wouldn't change for any amount of money now.

Gary Raynor

Brothers Together

Tottenham 'til I die? Well hopefully that will be a long time coming! My first match was a friendly against Sutton United at their ground in Surrey, when a relative who was a Director at Sutton took me.

That must have been about 1928 when I was 10 years old. My first memory of White Hart Lane shortly after was of going into what we called the Main Stand and seeing the freshly cut, green grass. I'd also never been in such a crowd. You see when you are brought up in the East End with only a brick back yard, it's things like the smooth pitch which I remember all those years ago.

Whatever happened, I became interested and would walk to Liverpool Street Station from where we lived in Heneage Street and get on the train to White Hart Lane. My twin brother and I would save our tuppence spending money so we could get the train which cost fourpence return. Entry into the ground was sixpence and a penny for the pink coloured programme. In those days, of course, it was steam trains and the journey was all part of the excitement of the day out as Spurs fans got on at Rectory Road and Stoke Newington – by the time we were at Stamford Hill the carriages were packed with standing room only. I was usually there at least an hour before kick-off and, while waiting in excited anticipation for the team to appear from behind the West Stand, we had the 'luxury', weather permitting, of being entertained by the local Enfield brass band, marching in formation and playing popular tunes of the day.

Many a time, when the ground was at full capacity and the crowd swell heaved dangerously forward, young nippers like myself would be lifted high above the heads of the supporters and tumbled down from hand to hand to the safety of the front to avoid crushing. When we arrived we would not head for the boys' enclosure but instead would go in where all the men were. Sometimes, because I was always quite short, the man at the turnstile would say to me to get down and crawl underneath so I got in free. I'd enjoy being a part of the growing crowd and catch all of the banter that spread along the terraces.

There were no sound systems of course, so if there was a change of player to the team that had been printed in the programme, a man would walk around the pitch holding a large blackboard with the name of the new player written in chalk. In later years, the management, in their wisdom, partitioned off a corner of the North Stand for children only, which was a wise and sensible decision.

I left school at 14 and went straight into a tailoring apprenticeship. My father was a shoemaker, specialising in making the uppers for women's shoes. He worked from home like many families around the Brick Lane area. Up to the age of 21 I made bespoke suits, eventually ending up in the West End in a garment maker's in Frith Street above a butcher's shop. The 1930s were the period of my youth and we would play clubs in the lower Divisions such as Chesterfield and Brentford. One player I remember from the early days, when I was about 12 years old, was David Levene who made a few appearances in the first team and who grew up in Bethnal Green just like me. It meant a lot to us that a young Jewish lad from where we were brought up had made it into the team.

My childhood heroes were players of the calibre we rarely see today. Attacking forwards like O'Callaghan and Willie Evans *[left]*, with the speed and skill that could outwit most defences. George Hunt, a centre-forward with bags of energy and determination that could be relied upon to score 30-plus goals season after season. Us fans had to wait two decades, until the 1950s when Bobby Smith joined the club, for a player like Hunt to be seen again.

Then, in defence, there were full-backs Channel and Whatley, with goalkeeper Nicholls behind them. Big, bold and brave, a man who was always safe and reliable. But the player who made Spurs so exciting to watch was the team captain, Arthur Rowe. A centre-half who changed the way the game should be played. Until he arrived on the scene centre-halves were called 'stoppers', who rarely moved out of their defence zone. His contribution to the 'push and run' era, from defence to attack, made Tottenham Hotspur the talk of the football world.

I was there when we played Sunderland in 1938 when I was 20 years old and it is reputed that 75,000 people attended, which I believe stands as a Club record to this day. Just two years before that many of us were amongst the huge crowd who went down to Cable Street one Sunday to prevent Oswald Mosley and his lot from marching through our area. Just the day before lots of us had been at White Hart Lane for a match against Sheffield United. Although I was small and couldn't get involved in the direct action we all felt we had to be there to offer our support.

We couldn't really afford to travel to away matches so lots of Spurs fans would go to Highbury on alternate Saturdays. Although there was rivalry between the two clubs it was always friendly.

Once I even took my rattle to a match when we were playing against Arsenal. When war was declared I got a six month deferral from the army as my boss said I was indispensable at the tailoring factory. You see I was making army uniforms. But then, after a series of postings I was amongst the infantry who were destined for the French/Belgian coast on D Day plus six. Or that was how it was intended.

But the weather was so bad we were sitting on the ships for six whole days before we could land. My twin brother, Harry, who is another very strong Tottenham supporter, went off to North Africa. We thought that there would be a better chance of one of us surviving if we separated. He saw action against Rommell in Libya and then into Italy. After we landed we came under gunfire and were told to dig trenches 10 yards apart. On the very first push forward six of my mates were killed when an enemy shell made a direct hit on their trench. So it was always a relief to return home on leave and come back to White Hart Lane for the War-time matches.

When I look back and think of highlights I suppose the Wembley Final against Leicester in 1961 is one of them. And the greatest player of them all? John White, who was so tragically struck by lightning. I liked his skilful style of play, a little like Tommy Harmer, who was always creating things during the game. Those memories will be with me forever. They say that history repeats itself and success follows success, so I'm looking forward to a bright and prosperous future!

Sid Tobias *pictured above with Harry on their 90th birthday and on previous pages as young boys*

Thanks For The Memories

Most of my greatest Spurs memories seem to feature the genius that was Glenn Hoddle – had this player come from any other nation then he would have been hailed as the greatest in the world – of that I have no doubt. His miraculous and uncanny skills with both feet were incredible and made a permanent impression in a young fan's memory. He was a midfield general that made every player around him flourish and I have a scrapbook full of tributes to Glenn from the likes of Cruyff, Maradona, Platini and Pele. You will not be surprised to hear that, to a man, they all stated what an exceptionally gifted player he was. Platini famously states that if Hoddle had been French, then he would have gained 150 caps and that he couldn't understand the English FA's mentality, especially their preoccupation with 'workrate' or 'crunch tackling' that got England precisely nowhere during the 1980s. As Spurs fans long realised, you build a team around someone with skill like Hoddle, players like him come along once in a generation, if you are lucky! Hoddle left Spurs for

Monaco, and under the leadership of Arsene Wenger, was voted French Player of the Year at a time when the French League was arguably the strongest in Europe. However, Glenn still could not get a regular place in the England team, the likes of Neil Webb seemingly being preferred. I believe we will never see the likes of Glenn again, at Tottenham or with three lions on his chest, and it is a depressing thought that the authorities failed to identify and nurture a talent like Glenn's. A failure that contributed to England's catalogue of failures. But thanks for the memories Glenn; at least Spurs fans know what an amazing player you were.

David Brooks *pictured with another Spurs legend, Cliff Jones*

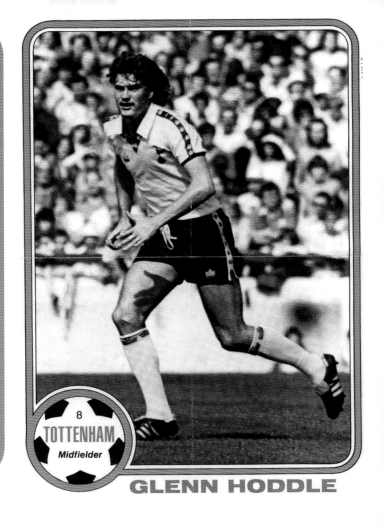

8
TOTTENHAM
Midfielder

GLENN HODDLE

Daddy's Girl

"COME ON YOU SPURS!" I have heard these four words repeated from the mouths of my father, grandfather and uncles ever since I can remember. My father grew up in North London and so it was natural for him and his brothers to support one of the leading local teams of the time and they decided to choose Tottenham ahead of their sworn rivals Arsenal.

Most of my friends cannot understand why I enjoy watching Spurs. The only apparent explanation to them is that I must have a crush on one of the players, but this is not the case. Although I can't exactly put my finger on why I feel so passionate about Spurs, it probably has a lot to do with the roller coaster of emotions that I feel before, during and after the match. The excitement and expectancy as we leave the car and walk towards the ground, the nervousness as we sit down on cold, plastic seats and the team is announced, the sense of hope as the two teams emerge to a cacophony of noise and the match begins, then the feeling of elation or deflation at the end of the match.

As we walk across the park on a dark winter's evening to White Hart Lane, there are swarms of people walking towards it, all with one aim in mind. As we walk down The Lane and the chant of, "COME ON YOU SPURS!" can be heard from all around the perimeter, the smell of burgers and onions and mounting excitement overwhelms me.

The huge crowds of Tottenham fans remind me of a modern day army or tribe, all united for one cause, desperate for one outcome. I love this feeling; it feels like one big family all wanting Spurs to emerge victorious. People from all backgrounds and social groups, people who would not normally talk to one another, find common ground within the stadium. I feel tied, bonded to all these people. We all love this team. Even though the board and the players have changed through the years, it is still the same club to us all. Through the highs and the lows the love affair never ends.

In a way Spurs has brought my father and me closer together. Our love of the boys at White Hart Lane and our regular visits, as season ticket holders, watching Spurs has given us a shared passion not experienced by all fathers and daughters. We share the experience and emotional roller coaster of being Spurs fans. I blame him for my addiction and great passion for this North London side.

Anna Gillespie *pictured with her dad at Wembley*

My Life Long Affair

My life long affair with Tottenham Hotspur began in the 1946/47 season. I am now in my 75th year and used to live in Harlow Village before it was developed into the New Town it is today. That season two school pals said that they were going to see Stanley Matthews, the George Best of the era, play for Stoke City in an FA Cup tie at White Hart Lane, so I went along with them to witness a 2-2 draw and I can still recite the whole Spurs team that day. Childhood memories are incredible, but they last you forever. One player who stood out was Ted Ditchburn, arguably the greatest goalie we've ever had, and we've had many good ones at Tottenham over the years. Anyway, my two friends never went again, but I was hooked!

After that I used to take my six-year-old brother to every home match, travelling on the train from Harlow to Northumberland Park on our own. The vast crowds were amazing to us young boys! In those days attendances were regularly over 40,000 and often topped 50,000. At the Cup tie against Stoke, more than 65,000 people somehow passed through the turnstiles! The crowd on the West Side swayed along the entire length of the pitch. I remember standing in the boys

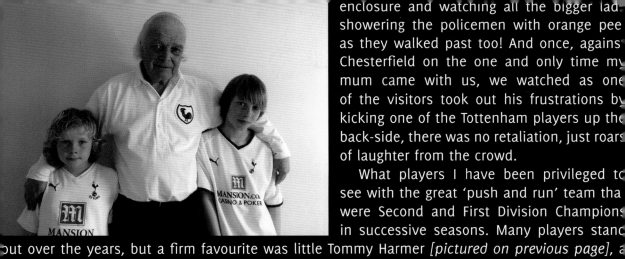

enclosure and watching all the bigger lads showering the policemen with orange peel as they walked past too! And once, against Chesterfield on the one and only time my mum came with us, we watched as one of the visitors took out his frustrations by kicking one of the Tottenham players up the back-side, there was no retaliation, just roars of laughter from the crowd.

What players I have been privileged to see with the great 'push and run' team that were Second and First Division Champions in successive seasons. Many players stand out over the years, but a firm favourite was little Tommy Harmer [pictured on previous page], a magician with the ball. Two years of National Service interrupted my Spurs attendance, but I was demobbed in 1956 and my family moved to Sussex. That proved no bar to my great enthusiasm to see the Lilywhites, because I used to travel to every home match from the south coast on my trusty Vespa scooter, a round trip of well over 100 miles in every kind of weather condition. Alfie Stokes and Johnny Brooks were my favourites at that time. Nowadays I derive my pleasure in taking my two young grandsons to the occasional game and they love the atmosphere at the Lane and look forward to building our new stadium. I also enjoy watching them play on Sunday mornings in the local youth leagues; what a truly great game football is.

Ken Nightingale *pictured above with his two grandsons*

PASS IT! PASS IT! PASS IT!

My earliest memory of watching Spurs was when we played Norwich in the League Cup Final in 1973. I was six years old and I remember sitting on the coach with my dad waiting to go home, holding a small plastic cup with blue and white ribbons that he had bought me. Dad told me to wave it at some Norwich fans who were sitting on the coach next to us, which I did. They didn't wave back!

Dad and I went to literally hundreds of matches together, but few more memorable than the Manchester City FA Cup Final replay, which ranks as one of the best nights of my life. And I never did let my dad live down the fact that he was screaming "PASS IT! PASS IT! PASS IT!" at Ricky Villa during the run that ended in the winning goal of winning goals!

We both missed out on a ticket for the League Cup Final against Liverpool in 1982. That was until dad nipped down to Tottenham High Road on the day of the game and bought me a ticket from a tout. I dread to think how much it cost him, but it was obviously so important to him that I was at the match.

My dad passed away a few years back and I've got a hell of a lot to thank him for, but most of all for introducing me to Tottenham Hotspur Football Club.

Nick Weston

TEN FOUR BIG BUDDY

When I reached the age of 60 just a few months ago, I was asked by my son-in-law if I remembered my first game at White Hart Lane. I told him that I was pretty sure that my grandfather took me when I was about six or seven as my dad worked on Saturdays, but I just couldn't remember the actual occasion. However, I did remember a memorable day not long afterwards, when I didn't make the game!

By October 1958 I had been to quite a few matches, getting the bus from Stamford Hill with my cousin Michael who was a year older – yes he was in charge of a ten-year-old at the ripe old age of 11! On the morning of 11 October that year, I remember talking to my dad before he went to work and he asked if I was going to the game. He didn't seemed to be at all worried that his young son and nephew went on their own to matches where the attendances were often over 50,000, with most of the spectators standing it was a real crush on the terraces but we always managed to wriggle our way to the front somehow. I told him it was up to Michael as we always went together and, as he was older than me, I took notice of what he said. Around lunchtime, I headed over the road to the block of flats in Clapton where Michael lived and asked him if we were going to the game. Because Spurs were having an average season he said he didn't really want to go – he was a bit flakey like that. Also, as it was only three days after his birthday and he'd been given a new football, he said he'd prefer to have a kick around in the playground. Even though I wanted to, I wasn't brave enough to go on my own, so I had to go along with his plans to play football rather than watch it at The Lane. Later that afternoon, as we wandered back to the block of flats were I lived, we saw a newspaper fluttering along the ground. Remember, this was way before the internet, or running scores on the TV or even full coverage on the radio, so there was no way of us lads knowing how the Spurs game was progressing until five o'clock when Sports Report on BBC Radio read out the results. However, the London evening newspapers, of which there were three, *The Standard*, *News* and *Star*, all printed various editions on a Saturday and there, lying on the ground in front of us, was one of the early editions.

On the back page was a 'Stop Press' column where the very latest news was added at the last second instead of missing the newspaper completely. We quickly picked up the stray newspaper and flicked straight to where the half-time scores had been inserted as the 'Stop Press'. To our horror, Spurs were beating Everton 6-1!! This was the famous day when Bill Nicholson took over the management of the team from Jimmy Anderson and Tottenham Hotspur rose to the occasion and ran out 10-4 winners.

Because of Michael's new football, we had missed the historic match and all the fun after the game surrounding that particular score-line. You see at that time *Highway Patrol* was one of the top TV programmes around and "10-4" was the programme's catch-phrase. As you may know it means "OK" in response to a message on the police in-car radio, and thousands of fans were leaving the ground saying "10-4" into pretend police radios with fake American accents!

Now, as a season ticket holder for over 35 years, having attended over 1000 home games, I can only look back and regret that the game against Everton back in 1958 wasn't one of them. I've never let Michael, who is now a regular at The Lane, forget that day and, for his 60th birthday, to commemorate the occasion, I presented him with a framed programme from that fateful Everton match!

Alan Fitter *pictured [left] with cousin Michael Tenzer and a programme from the missed match*

JIMMY'S LAST GAME

I made my Spurs debut as a supporter on a September evening in 1964, witnessing a 2-1 win over Stoke City at White Hart Lane. It goes without saying that one James P. Greaves [pictured] was on the score-sheet that night. If Spurs scored invariably Greaves would be netting at least one of them and a brace or hat-trick were common occurrences. Diminutive in stature, Jimmy Greaves was a giant among marksmen and is arguably the greatest goal-scorer the British game has ever seen, most certainly in the post-War era. Back in the Sixties there simply wasn't the intense hype or scrutiny that marks today's game, but in his day, Greaves was the icon that, in recent times, we have witnessed with the likes of Shearer and Owen.

Over the next few seasons I watched 'Gentleman Jim' score goals aplenty as Bill Nicholson set about building another fine team to replace the historic 'Double' side of a few years earlier. Then, in the 1969/70 season a strange thing happened. As Tottenham languished in mid-table following indifferent form, the goals started to dry up for Greaves. Shockwaves ran through the club when we were dumped out of the Cup by lowly Crystal Palace on a cold January night at Selhurst Park and, as a consequence, Kinnear, Knowles, Gilzean, and yes, even Jimmy Greaves were dropped from the team. A brilliant up and coming youngster by the name of Perryman was also rested having put in some amazing displays following his debut the previous September. Sadly Greavsie the goal-getting genius was, unlike the others, never to regain his place in the team and it was quite by chance that I saw his final game in our colours.

As I arrived at Victoria station, bound for our match against Leeds United on Valentine's Day 1970, a large blackboard announced, "Spurs v Leeds MATCH OFF". I assumed this was due to the icy conditions, so I made tracks to Highbury where I knew the reserve team was playing Arsenal. Imagine my horror when at half-time the Tannoy system announced the latest score from White Hart Lane, where Spurs were playing after all! Despite a side packed with first team regulars, the Spurs reserves went down 2-0 and, to add insult to injury, Greaves was booked for one of the few times in his career. Such an ignominious end for one of the greatest players ever seen in a Spurs shirt.

Graham Bishop

TO THE BITTER END

My love affair with Tottenham Hotspur began as a seven-year-old on 10 September 1988. In the old First Division it was the home club who appointed the reserve official for their games and as a senior member of the North Middlesex Referees' Society my dad, Peter, was often selected for duty at White Hart Lane.

It was during one of these games, against Arsenal, that he brought me along for the first time. It was equally memorable and special as the game marked Gazza's home debut and the boy wonder became an instant crowd favourite by scoring a quite incredible goal. Gazza's goal was notable for the fact that as he took the ball past the Arsenal defenders his boot came off and so he scored with his sock half way off his foot. This was featured in all of the papers and he became an instant hero with the fans.

However, the game was to end on a bitter note from this young fan's perspective and ended with a score line I have never, and will never, accept as the true one. According to the record books Arsenal "won" 3-2. But in the last few minutes Vinny Samways looked to have equalised when he drilled home a close range shot past John Lukic. I had jumped up and celebrated with the majority of fans inside the stadium, but was inconsolable when told by a friend's dad, who I was sitting with while dad was on duty, that the goal had been disallowed for a phantom offside decision. I've got the end of season video, which shows all the action of the season and Samways was at least level with the Arsenal defender when he received the ball. Ever since that day I have told people that the game had ended in a 3-3 draw and I will never truly accept otherwise.

To add insult to injury, if that goal had been awarded, which it should have been, then Arsenal would have had two less points and would therefore not have been able to manage to pull off that dramatic, last gasp, title win at Anfield that season. Without that win Arsenal would have also lost a whole generation of fans and Nick Hornby would not have written that book. If only the linesman in the derby match at White Hart Lane had tweaked a hamstring or twisted an ankle, because my dad would have stepped in – dad would never have flagged for offside!

My luck wasn't all out though, after the final whistle had blown and all the fans had left White Hart Lane to make their way home, I was taken round to the front entrance to wait for my dad to finish getting changed, and it was on my way there that I found a £1 coin. At the time £1 was double my weekly pocket money. So first game, a 3-3 draw versus Arsenal, Gazza's debut, and a quid up! Not a bad beginning, eh?!?

Gareth Dace *pictured with his dad*

MY HOUSE RULES

My father was a devout Spurs supporter so naturally I followed my dad and began supporting the best team in the world – Tottenham Hotspur! I am very passionate about Spurs and I am proud to say that I have a Spurs flag which is majestically displayed on the wall in my hallway. I love the way that the cockerel stands on top of the football looking very regal and superior and it should be admired, respected, valued and appreciated. I have a rule that you need to show your respect and admiration for my beloved team's emblem, which is very visible to anyone entering my flat. A simple but very effective way of displaying this is to bow down to my Spurs flag when passing it. All of my family and friends are fully aware of my rule and anyone who is socially visiting my flat needs to respect my request of bowing to the flag. If a visitor forgets to show appreciation for my flag by bowing down to it, then I quickly and firmly demand that they "bow to the cockerel!" There are no exceptions to my rule and regardless of what football team you support, you still need to honour it. Any visitors who refuse to bow to my flag will not be able to proceed to the comfort of my living room and they will be denied the pleasure of experiencing my wonderful hospitality! It goes without saying that I have yet to be visited by friends who are Arsenal supporters! They say that they refuse to bow to the Spurs cockerel due to the fact that we are notorious rival supporters. Could the reason possibly be that they are scared to recognise and admit our superiority as the best team in London? The one and only Tottenham Hotspur! Come on you Spurs!!!

Michelle Dolan *pictured with her bowing Manchester United supporting friend Emma*

LEONARD STANLEY DUQUEMIN - SPURS

THE DAY WE MET THE DUKE OF GUERNSEY

Born in 1930 I started coming to The Lane with my dad and uncle Titch in 1937. A little after this period, in the 1940s, my friends and I would hang about the ground after games for the players to emerge so we would collect their autographs on scraps of paper, a programme or, if we were very lucky, an autograph book. I collected almost all of the team.

Many of the players at that time were in the Services and we used to follow them along the High Road to Bruce Grove station where they would catch their trains, returning to their barracks or airfields. That 40's team was full of top class players; Ted Ditchburn, Ronnie Burgess, Les Medley, Eddie Baily and Alf Ramsey. All internationals and all playing for Tottenham. I got all their autographs, except for my special hero, The Duke, Len Duquemin. He was a good looking man, with slicked back hair, broad shoulders and a muscular build. Not the quickest, but a great header of the ball and a canon ball shot. Len was a very hard worker for the team who never stopped running and, in doing so, scored over 100 goals for Tottenham. For me, he was the bee's knees. I never saw him off the pitch, which was a big disappointment.

By the summer of 1948, I was in the Royal Navy and my ship visited the Channel Islands. I went ashore with a fellow Spurs fan, Shiner Wright, for a quiet pint. We found the pub which I had read about in St. Peter Port called The White Hart. What else? The landlord was called Ted Zabiela and was the man responsible for The Duke leaving the islands for The Lane. After introducing ourselves, to our delight, Ted told us that Len Duquemin was expected in that evening. So, one pint became two and later the door opened and in walked The Duke.

We spent the rest of the evening together, chatting about football in general and, of course, Spurs in particular! Len was a modest man and avoided blowing his own trumpet; instead he was full of praise for his teammates. I was still suffering from the disappointment of watching our lads losing in extra time in the semi final of the Cup to Blackpool and I said to Len, "Will we go to Wembley this year?" His reply was, "We are going to concentrate on winning promotion". And of course we did, quite easily, with The Duke playing some great football along the way.

That achievement was part of building the foundations for the wonderful team that followed. Just as importantly, I did get his autograph after all, a signed photograph that I still have to this day. I am in a wheelchair now but still come to every home game with my son.

Larry Cotton

An Exhausting Journey

I recall with mixed feelings a trip to Newcastle on 21 January 1976 for a League Cup semi-final, second leg – Spurs had won the first leg 1-0 at White Hart Lane. We set out for the long journey north on the morning of the match in my 1500GT Ford Cortina. Having reached the other side of London without too many traffic jams, I was confident of arriving at our destination in good time.

Unfortunately, 200 miles from Newcastle, we heard a very loud bang and smoke started pouring from the engine bay. I pulled over to the side of the road and my mechanic mate checked the damage. He said it didn't look good as we were only firing on three pistons and the fourth had blown! Distraught and with immediate thoughts of the game in mind, I chugged onto the forecourt of a garage 500 yards up the road. There I spoke to an AA chap and asked him to inspect the engine for me. He confirmed that only three pistons were working and that the engine may be cracked – he suggested we leave the car there while he arranged for a pick-up truck to take it home with us. Tentatively, I asked if there was 'any chance' of the car being driven to Newcastle at which he just burst out laughing, saying that we would be lucky if we managed a mile let alone 200!

I slowly wandered back to the car and sheepishly relayed the news about the engine to the three passengers. Everybody was gutted for me as I was the only 'true' Spurs fan in the car. The two friends and my brother had asked to travel for day out purposes and the experience of witnessing a major football match. And that's when I stunned them and told them I had decided to push on in the Cortina anyway – I was hell-bent on getting there somehow. So, regardless of all the mechanical advice, off we set again with smoke seeming to pour from every part of the car. Other road users were tooting and flashing at us, some very enthusiastically, to let me know there was a problem with the vehicle! I politely waved to acknowledge these caring drivers, but the majority probably didn't see me through the thick black smoke. So, did we make it to Newcastle? Of course we did! Although driving around the many roundabouts and through the town centre really was a sight for sore eyes, not to mention the sound of hooters being blown in our direction!

As for the match itself, hopes were high after the first leg victory, but alas, it all turned sour on the night. Newcastle's Alan Gowling scored the first with only three minutes on the clock, Keeley headed home a corner kick a minute into the second-half, then, with just over an hour gone, Cassidy measured a pass to perfection across the Spurs box and found Nulty who drove the ball into the net to make the score 3-0 on the night. For some reason this appeared to spark Spurs into life, as two minutes later McAllister headed in from a Pratt corner to reduce the arrears.

This could have been 'game on', but despite John Duncan sending a shot from two yards the wrong side of the post, the score remained the same. Absolutely gutted I made my way back to the car with flashbacks of the game clear in my mind and what might have been. My friends, although disappointed for me, had other matters on their mind, namely the journey home. Although I understood their concerns, the long trek back was overridden in my thoughts by the sadness at missing out on a Wembley final. It's sad but very true! After another very 'smoky' drive, we arrived home tired and exhausted nine hours later. Shortly afterwards, a few of us fitted a reconditioned engine – on a day when Spurs didn't have a game!

Phil Brackstone

SO MANY MEMORIES

Born and bred in Enfield, there really is only one team – The Lilywhites! My dear old dad, unfortunately no longer with us, used to take me and my elder brother along to White Hart Lane when we were youngsters and I can still remember him telling me, when I was just six years old to, "Stop swinging around the bars!" These were of course the crowd control bars on the terracing, not those I have since grown very fond of!

I can remember dad telling me that when he was a youngster his favourite player was our No.1, Ted Ditchburn. Dad used to stand behind the goal watching the game intently and, as the opposition attacked, he would tell Ted to, "Go to the left Ted" or "Go to the right Ted", depending on which wing the attacks were coming down. Apparently one day Ted turned to my dad, obviously fed up with being told how to defend our goal, and said, "Why don't you bloody well shut up!?!". Dad was a little taken aback as you can imagine, but he always did like to talk a lot. Anyway, I think that my dad's coaching had a big bearing on the success that Ted went on to have in our goal! He was pivotal in Arthur Rowe's famous 1950-51 'push and run' side, a team that my dad always said was, "The best that he had ever seen".

Dad also took me along to the League Cup Final against Aston Villa in 1971 and, being on the short side still, he had made me a stool to stand on. Kitted out in blue 'n white, with a huge rosette pinned to my chest, there I stood proud as Punch atop my stool. Then Big Chiv stuck one in the net and the terraces erupted. I was launched head long from my stool amid wild celebrations and ended up almost ten rows down the terracing. Dad picked me up, brushed me down, wiped away my tears of joy and pain, then plonked me back on my stool. When Chiv got another, I think you can guess what happened again!

[Above centre] *Brian at the Spurs training ground with Steve Perryman [left] and Martin Chivers*
[Left] *Brian with Spurs hero Gary Mabbutt*

The majority of my years supporting the team as a youngster were spent on the famous 'Shelfside'. Memories of days spent on the Shelf still send a shiver down my spine; what a fantastic place to stand and watch my beloved Tottenham. No other club in the country had an area of terracing quite like it. I will always look back with fond memories of the choruses of "What do ya wanna make those eyes at me for?" whilst standing on the terracing; transferring to the front of the Shelf from the back after a round of "Knees up Mother Brown", my hair dripping with beer that was sent flying in the process. Fantastic support. One match that springs to mind was our Second Leg UEFA Cup Final win against Wolverhampton Wanderers, when Tra La La La Mullery stuck a header into the back of the Wolves net (and got knocked out in the process) to ensure that we took the trophy in 1972.

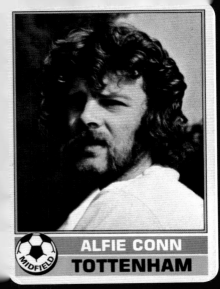

ALFIE CONN
TOTTENHAM
MIDFIELD

I can remember turning up at The Lane hours before kick off to be sure of getting a good place right at the front of The Shelf. Following the game I walked all the way back to Enfield, singing choruses of Tottenham songs, rattle in hand, with my silk scarf tied to my head and another tied to my wrist. Another memorable occasion was our Second Leg UEFA Cup Final game against Anderlecht in 1984 when Robbo stuck the ball into the back of the net very late into the game, sending the Final to penalties. Tony Parks was playing in goal on the night, while our skipper, Stevie Perryman, was suspended. Parksie performed heroics, saving the vital penalties, sending us all into raptures. Tottenham High Road was packed after the game, celebrations in full swing. Happy days!

It broke my heart when The Shelf was replaced. I can remember having a sit-in on The Shelf following a home game and becoming part of the SOS (Save our Shelf) campaign. Unfortunately, the inevitable happened and The Shelf was replaced when all-seater stadiums became the norm, although the slight remnants of the old stand can still be recognised in front of the executive boxes in the East Stand.

And we've had some fantastic players in my time following Spurs; although I have to admit my favourite is Alfie Conn. In 1975, with the threat of relegation looming large, Alfie *[pictured above]* was truly majestic in guiding us to a 4-2 win in our final home game against Leeds United. Unfortunately the reprieve lasted just two more years.

A year spent in Division Two could, by many, have been considered a bit of a disaster, but oh what season it was!! I can remember the last home game from the previous campaign when we were

Spurs fans on the pitch following the club's relegation to Division Two

already relegated, but the support from the terracing was magnificent; buzzing with talk that we would soon return to our rightful place in the top flight. And Jimmy Holmes stuck away a beauty that day. I had an evening job working on the turnstiles at the old Haringey Stadium in Green Lanes, but still found time to get onto the pitch at the end of the game, tearing the seam on my trousers wide open in the process, before rushing off to work.

I attended most games, home and away, in the Second Division season and our support would turn up in thousands, taking over towns in a carnival atmosphere. It was a real novelty to go to different places and play against sides like Bristol Rovers, Notts County, Brighton, Blackpool and Oldham – to name but a few. I used to go to the away games with the Spurs Supporters' Club, which used to be based in Warmington House to the right hand side of the main front entrance to the stadium. I also remember that famous piece of graffiti announcing that, "Ken Dodd's Dad's Dogs Dead", which was painted on the wall by the entrance to the Supporters Club for a number of years. For the shorter journeys myself and my mates travelled by coach. Spurs used to use the old Grey-Green coach company, which was situated behind The Globe public house at the Angel Edmonton.

Grey-Green coaches, from personal experience, always seemed to have problems with their fleet. I can recall attending a game away to Coventry, which should have been only a couple of hours up the motorway, however, we unfortunately broke down around the Rugby area, and waited by the side of the motorway for a replacement coach to take us the remaining ten or so miles onto Highfield Road. When we eventually got to the ground the game was already 30 minutes old, the score was 1-1 (with Peter Taylor apparently getting our goal) and nothing much else happened for the remaining 60 minutes. After the game we, along with thousands of other Spurs supporters, were escorted back to the coach park. One by one the coaches came and went until there was just our coach-load of supporters left, but no coach! We were eventually given a lift to Rugby train station where we were left to board a train back to London.

On the away game to Blackpool we opted for the 'Football Special' instead, leaving from one of London's main line train stations. Along with my mate, Tony Tomling, I sat in a compartment with a couple of older supporters. I can remember one of the older lads getting out a bottle of whisky and offering Tony and I a swig, which we declined. By the time we arrived at Blackpool Station the two other lads were completely out of it and fast asleep in the carriage. We were unable to wake them and to this day I don't know if they made the game at all. By the look of them, I very much doubt it!

Another unforgettable game in that season was our 9-0 home win against Bristol Rovers. Spurs had just signed Colin Lee from Torquay and he went on to bag four goals on the day, with our much ridiculed striker Ian Moores also getting a hat-trick. We almost undid all of our hard work in trying to gain promotion towards the end of the season with away defeats to our closest rivals at the time, Brighton & Hove Albion and Bolton Wanderers. I can recall walking into the ground at Bolton before the game and the Tannoy was playing the Queen hit *We are the Champions*, with both sets of supporters bellowing out the words as if their lives depended on it. It all came down to our final game, away to Southampton, at the old Dell. We were packed in like sardines and I could only get the odd glimpse of the goal that we were standing behind. The game finished 0-0, Spurs regained their place in the First Division, and we all enjoyed a very happy journey home!

Then there was the FA Cup tie at Swindon in January 1980 where we were given an area of terracing behind one goal. Towards the rear left-hand side of the stand there was a refreshment hut selling hot dogs and dodgy looking burgers, which caught my eye because thick black smoke was billowing from that direction. It wasn't long before the stall was engulfed in flames and the fire brigade turned up – the hamburgers were well done too! There are so many great memories and I'm sure many more are yet to come in the years ahead. *Glory, Glory, Hallelujah!!!*

Alan Gifford

CHAS & DAVE & SUE TOO

Because I'd spent most of my early life living abroad, I didn't come back to England until I was 15, I was a bit of a late starter as far as Spurs were concerned. But life changed for me one Saturday when my dad said he was taking me to a football match. I have to be honest and admit that I didn't want to go – like a lot of 16-year-old girls, I was more into makeup and boys than football, but nevertheless, I was dragged reluctantly along. My apathy was short lived though; I loved it at White Hart Lane.

Although I didn't get the chance to go again until many years later, I always followed the team's progress in the papers, as in those days there wasn't much football on telly. Anyway, I left home, got married and had children then, one day, 17 years later, I was out shopping with a friend of mine who lived at Chase Lodge, the training ground that Spurs moved to in 1988. Her husband, who was the groundsman there, came over to say hello while I was dropping her off and, after a brief chat during which I told him I was looking for a job, he told me they were looking for a new cook at the training ground – he asked if I'd be interested. I jumped at the chance to be considered, so he took me over to meet Terry Venables who gave me the job there and then. I started work for Tottenham Hotspur on 1 August 1988; the day a bomb went off in the barracks at Mill Hill and killed all those poor soldiers. I worked at Chase Lodge for seven years before the club moved the players to the new training ground at Chigwell.

One of the early highlights from working there was when I met my hero Gary Lineker – yes even us oldies have crushes. I remember watching him in the 1986 World Cup when he won the Golden Boot; so you can imagine my excitement when I heard he was coming to Spurs. I didn't get to meet Gary until he had been there three days, and I remember Gary Mabbutt coming over and asking if I'd been introduced yet? When I said no, he smiled and disappeared. The next thing I knew Gary was standing in front of me saying hello. I was totally tongue-tied and it took about a week for me to realise that he was actually a human like the rest of us. I tried not to have favourite players, but I have to admit I did have a soft spot for Gazza. He wrote about me in his *Daft as a Brush* book and he came over to me every morning to say hello and to give me a kiss.

But my very best Spurs memories are reserved for the FA Cup run in 1991, in particular the Semi against Arsenal at Wembley. That was my first match at Wembley and I couldn't wait. What a fantastic day, which included a match that I still regard as the best I have ever been to. I have watched the video about ten times since and I never tire of the memories. After the match we dropped our friends off at the training ground and decided to wait for the players to come back and congratulate them. As they arrived they hugged and kissed me and we were jumping up

and down – they were so happy. Over the next few weeks the training ground was buzzing with excitement ahead of the Cup Final against Nottingham Forest.

When the big day finally arrived, my husband and I drove to White Hart Lane, where the club had laid on breakfast for us as well as coaches to Wembley. I just wanted to get to the stadium and sing *Abide With Me* as it was something I always wanted to do – I cried when we sang it.

The match was ok, not as good as the Semi, but it was totally spoilt when Gazza was injured – I was so worried about him. We watched with great pride as the boys went up to collect the Cup – Princess Diana was there and I have a great photo of Gary Mabutt holding up the trophy with Diana behind him clapping. Then the fun began!

We had to get a train back to Stanmore as, believe it or not, I was appearing in my children's school concert as one of the Beverly Sisters. After my appearance we rushed home where I quickly got changed, before rushing off to the Hilton Hotel in a taxi for the club's celebration party. Following the Champagne Reception we all went in the ballroom for dinner, after which the music started. Chas and Dave were in full flow when all the team got on the stage to sing with them. I was standing near the back watching when the late, great Ken Wolstenholme saw me. Ken was a regular visitor to the training ground and always came in to say hello and get a cup of tea, but I couldn't believe it when he pushed me towards the front where David Howells and Paul Walsh then grabbed my hands and pulled me up on stage with them. I couldn't believe it, there I was on stage with all the players and Chas and Dave singing *When the year ends in one*. Well, I just had to sing along with them didn't I?

I am proud to say that I support Spurs – the happy memories outweigh the sad ones and not many fans can say they have had their photos taken with the FA Cup, League Cup and Charity Shield. All I need to add to my collection is the Champions League trophy. Maybe next year!

Sue Franklin *pictured on stage with the players and on previous page with Jurgen Klinsmann*

THOSE WERE THE DAYS

For those who missed the vast, open, White Hart Lane terraces of old, ours was an entirely different football experience to today's more controlled, homogenized environment. With few ticket implications and a liquid, though volatile crowd, Sixties, Seventies and Eighties supporters could go where time, choice and money dictated, while witnessing some of the most incredible scenes and memories known to man. Truth is, the entire experience represented a living, breathing fantasy, while the humour and camaraderie will never leave heart or mind.

Saturdays were simply sacred – pre paid TV days – while the faces, characters and players that peppered our terrace lives made the bad times worth living. Jennings, Kinnear and Knowles were the beginning of our Tottenham mantra, knowing more about their lives than those of our very own parents! Drawn to the Nicholson flame by a plethora of flamboyant, white-shirted heroes, each and every game was prefaced by a swirling upsurge of anticipation as the Mullery, Mackay and Greaves returned our raucous adulation with a turning, overhead clap at the end of their personally delivered acclaim. Terrace choir and team joined as one, although I often wondered how Gilly, Mike England or Beally perceived some of the off-field shenanigans of their fans.

I remember seeing signs for the outskirts of Southampton, the traditional songs and posturing heralding one of many grand entrances to another football stronghold. Traffic was jammed as far as the eye could see, but, amazingly, the entire Hampshire Police force was driving AWAY from the city! In fact, there were so many flashing blue lights and sirens, that it momentarily distracted our attention from the approaching ground. Pre-mobile phones, the incredibly accurate match-day tom-tom's went into full overdrive. It soon transpired that a band of rogue Spurs fans had 'borrowed' up to 30 Corporation milk floats and were driving them around town in an unofficial attempt at the world's largest and longest dodgem ride! It wasn't particularly clever, or bright, but was typical of the fantastic humour of boys escaping the seriousness of life, while releasing the pressure valve of their comparatively humdrum days. Nobody was hurt, although a few pints were quickly turned to yoghurt in the ensuing chase, political correctness a twinkle in the eye of future darkening days.

Often, out of the threat of trouble, came humour from adversity. Tottenham v Chelsea has always been my personal Cup Final as a south London-based disciple of the famous, crowing cockerel; Arsenal merely considered 'some team from over the river', with a penchant for over-starching the sleeves of their shirts.

In the days of the infamous Park Lane being split into two, the rival sets of London protagonists grew ever closer, ever threatening. I was no more than 13 and wedged behind a huge, unshaven, abuse-spitting man, with a cigarette stub attempting to escape from his angry lips. In yet another tirade of threats, his stub flew up in to the air. I was scared, yet intrigued, and remained in his shadow, comparatively safe from the baying aggression of the crowd. Eventually, one of those infamous terrace gaps developed, with the remainder of the crowd convinced that the inevitable fight had started. It hadn't! Nor had his cigarette stub made the ground, but had lodged inside his turn-up and slowly caught fire. For those who've ever seen a similar scene in *One Flew Over The Cuckoo's Nest*, you'll appreciate the humour more than most, which instantly killed the impending threat of trouble. The thought of hundreds of skinhead Tottenham fans trying to douse his leg will live with me forever, with donkey jackets flying through the air with gusto, and a constant trickle of St. John's Ambulance and Police hats rolling down the dispersing terrace. Whatever the rules of life, they'll never take the memory of our football humour away!

Tottenham Hotspur: The class of '77

Even now, I am still haunted by the grisly reality of relegation, with every blade of home turf hidden by a sea of defiant bodies. ''We'll be back again next year!'' they chanted, as hundreds, probably thousands clambered up into the seats of the, now departed Directors. And true to our promise, we returned the very next season [77-78], with a final day point, again at Southampton, securing our return to top-flight football. That day, the incredible force of Tottenham togetherness came to bear, with hundreds dressed up in celebratory fancy dress.

I recall encountering three bearded nurses from Walthamstow! As we all blended into the crowd, we merged with a group of laughing Vikings who had swapped a day of pillage by parking their overheated Reliant Robin in Tesco's car park. Shouting our goodbyes, we exchanged a few brief words with Mickey and Minnie Mouse – now apparently residents of Stevenage – and wished good luck to a band of skipping St. Trinian's schoolgirls who were chanting Tottenham songs with Elvis Presley and Rod Stewart in tow. Yes, it could be said that the girl with the hairy chest and beer gut looked decidedly dodgy, but so what?

They were Tottenham! And above all the bobbing heads in that busy, unforgettable scene, was a huge Donald Duck head that wobbled all the way to the old Dell, with the home fans left wondering what had happened to their ordered City. In the passing of time, I'll never forget those who climbed to the top of the Lane's floodlights, or those who proudly draped our colours across everyday life. Or my mate, Jerry, picking up hundreds of coins that had rained down from a northern terrace. Short on work and hope, yet thankful to the angry hordes who, unbeknown to them, had kindly paid for his return journey home!

The terraces were our life; alive and buzzing and full of the unique Tottenham vitality that we'll take to our graves. Incredibly, our togetherness, our camaraderie and spirit, has grown in adversity. You can keep your Uniteds, Citys, Rangers and Rovers. As they say, ''We are Tottenham, super Tottenham'' and

Not Quite The Same Any More

With a Spurs mad brother, John, and a teacher, George Robb, it was only natural that I would follow in their footsteps and become an ardent fan too. My first game was certainly memorable – the 2-1 home defeat to West Bromwich Albion on the final day of the famous Double winning season. I saw Danny Blanchflower raise the League trophy high above his head and in the 48 subsequent years have, sadly, never seen it repeated.

Then, in 1986, the family tradition was passed down another generation when I took my son, Christopher, to see his first match – ironically a 5-0 victory against West Bromwich Albion. He soon became a season ticket holder and travelled the length and breadth of the country watching his beloved Spurs, until tragedy struck.

In August 2005 Chris was diagnosed with Burkitt Lymphoma, a rare and particularly aggressive blood cancer. With remarkable courage he faced his illness head on, determined to defeat the disease. His friends rallied round and they were helped in no small way by his beloved Spurs.

Gary Mabbutt paid two visits, both to our home and then again to his hospital ward, then Chris and I spent a never-to-be-forgotten day as a guest of Gary Lineker in the *Match of the Day* studios and finally, he was able to watch the first team train and met Martin Jol in person.

Sadly, on 12 July 2006, at the young age of 26, Chris died, but I will treasure these moments that we shared at Tottenham. Now, three years later, I still go to White Hart Lane – I've seen over 1250 Spurs matches since that day back in 1961 – but it's not quite the same any more.

I gave up my season ticket and now sit in Christopher's seat instead. I wore his Spurs shirt to Wembley and was probably the only supporter who shed tears of sadness when Spurs beat Chelsea in the Carling Cup Final. Chris would have loved that day, but life for me must go on and one of my last promises to my son was that I would always give Spurs a cheer for him so... "Come On You Spurs!"

Geoff Niblett *pictured with Martin Jol and Gary Mabbutt*

A MEMORIAL FUND HAS BEEN SET UP IN CHRISTOPHER'S NAME TO RAISE MONEY FOR THE TREATMENT OF BURKITT LYMPHOMA IN DEVELOPING COUNTRIES

SIR'S A SPUR

It all began on a balmy spring evening in April 1958 and a friendly fixture against Hibernian. Hibs were regular visitors to White Hart Lane in the 1950s and on this occasion they were warming up for the Scottish Cup final against Clyde a few days later. The reason for my first visit to The Lane, however, had its origins at Summers Lane, the home of Finchley FC, at the time a successful amateur side in the Athenian League. My father and I were regular supporters and Finchley's star player of the era was a fast, stocky, rather bandy-legged left-winger named George Robb. Robb had signed as an amateur for Spurs in 1951 and then, well into his twenties, signed professional forms in 1953. George was followed into the Finchley side by a fleet-footed young winger, Jeff Ireland, who also signed professional forms for Tottenham in 1957. For the Hibernian fixture, Robb was on the left-wing and Ireland on the right and both players duly scored in a 4-0 win. Little did I appreciate from my vantage point on the Shelf that this would be the first of over 950 visits to White Hart Lane. During the past 50 years I have been lucky to see a number of outstanding wingers wearing a Spurs shirt from the electric Cliff Jones, the accurate Terry Dyson, the unselfish Tony Galvin, the mesmeric Chris Waddle to the hugely entertaining David Ginola. But few can surpass George Robb's goal-scoring record from the wing. In 200 league and cup games he scored 58 times, a most impressive tally. While still playing for Spurs, George Robb was a schoolteacher at Christ's College, Finchley where I was a pupil. His talents were not confined to wing play and scoring goals, however, as I recall to my cost. For obvious reasons in the Masters v School match he was banned from playing as an outfield player, so he went in goal – and saved my penalty!

John Abbott pictured above with his father (left) George Robb with the ball and Christ's schoolmasters

OLDER, WISER, SADDER

I was something of a late-comer to Spurs, being more interested in books and Barbie than Crooks and Archibald, but nine years ago there was a spare ticket going and I decided to tick 'live football match' off my list of things to experience. The game was Tottenham versus Newcastle, the score 4-2 to Spurs. I didn't know it, but George Graham was in charge, and the pulsating encounter included three sendings off, three penalties and six goals – that was about as exciting as it ever got under the man in the raincoat.

Players flitted before my eyes... Rebrov, Anderton, Doherty, Clemence. I didn't have the faintest idea who any of them were. I didn't know a corner kick from a throw-in and the waves of chanting from the stands had me completely baffled and struggling to make out the words. But the atmosphere – the icy January evening, the floodlit pitch and the electric charge in the stands caught me right in the gut and I was transfixed. I got so carried away I ended up screeching, "Get it out! Get it out!" the minute the ball got within five yards of the Spurs penalty area. My brother pretended he didn't know me. I bought my first season ticket 18 months later.

I'm older, wiser and sadder nowadays; I've seen the highs of victory, of beautiful and creative football; I've seen the lows of defeat and the ignominy of that 3-4 Cup replay against Manchester City. I now know exactly what a corner is and, like a seasoned supporter, have come to dread the opposition's ones. But nothing will ever quite compare to that very first time when, with the scent of grass and fried onions on the cold night air, I witnessed Spurs scoring four and White Hart Lane rocking in response.

Sonya Lipczynska *pictured at White Hart Lane*

PLAYER'S CIGARETTES

CLAY · McDONALD
HUNTER
SMITH · GRIMSDELL
WALTERS
BANKS · DIMMOCK
SEED · CANTRELL · BLISS

ASSOCIATION CUP WINNERS
TOTTENHAM HOTSPUR. 1921

Dad's First Cup Final

"It was nine o'clock in the morning on Saturday, 23 April, 1921 when three young lads started out on our big adventure. Two of us were 11 and one 14 years old. We each had a haversack packed with two fish paste and two jam sandwiches, a bottle of water, and the grand total of £1.4s.0d in pre-decimal money between us, which works out to around £1.20 in today's terms. After walking from our homes in Bethnal Green to Liverpool Street station, we caught a train to Parsons Green, which was the nearest station to Stamford Bridge at the time. We arrived at the ground at about 11.30am, ate our sandwiches and along with the thousands of others supporters, waited for the gates to open at about one o'clock. We paid 2s.6d (12p) to get in and got as near as we could to the pitch. I regret to say, being small, I saw very little of the game, but the thrill was in just being there. When Jimmy Dimmock scored the only goal of that game against Wolves, it seemed that everyone went mad. What a day! Tired and hungry we arrived home at around six in the evening, happy that our Spurs had won the Cup. I'll never forget the Spurs team that day: Hunter, Clay,

McDonald, Smith, Walters, Grimsdell, Banks, Bliss, Cantrell, Seed, Dimmock."

My dad, Fred Jordan, *[pictured above front row far left]* was a lifelong Spurs fan who passed away in 1994, aged 84. At some point shortly before he died, he wrote down the above for his grandson, Nic. He is now 32 and also a life-long Spurs supporter and season ticket holder, so the family tradition that spans back almost a century carries on into the future.

Dave Jordan

Mama Dandolo & Co

We moved to Tottenham in 1955, the day after mum, Maroulla, came out of Charing Cross Hospital having given birth to my younger brother. We were the first Cypriot family in the area. My parents were already big football fans from their days in Cyprus, but now there was only one team to support - our beloved Spurs.

Dad worked on Saturdays, so when my brothers were old enough, mum [known to everyone as Mama Dandolo] would take the three of us kids to White Hart Lane where we would stand on the terraces over on the Shelf side. Many a time mum and I would get up in the middle of the night to queue up at White Hart Lane for FA Cup tickets, often in the freezing cold.

As mum grew older, she started suffering from osteoporosis, which affected her ability to get to matches, but she still enjoyed watching Spurs on TV. Due to her condition, by the time she reached her mid-70s, an already little lady of under 5ft had shrunk by another six inches as her spine had bent. Dressed in black, as she was a Cypriot widow, and walking with a stick, she surprised me one day when she told me that she would like to go to White Hart Lane once more. She hadn't been inside the all-seater stadium, nor seen the large screens, but I'm pleased to say she made it and loved seeing her team win again.

Not long before mum died in 2006, at the age of 85, I was on my way to a Spurs game and popped in to see her at the care-home where she was living. Mum could no longer walk, was very frail and had Alzheimer's. After a chat I told her where I was going and, in a rare lucid moment, she said, "Can I come with you?" Tottenham 'til she died.

Myrna Hughes

[Photo back left to right] Myrna, Mama, Jack & Tom with and friends setting out for the Lane

CAPTIVATED
BY THE CLUB'S
TRADITIONS

t is not just Tottenham 'til I die; it is Tottenham even when I'm long gone. That's the same fo all true Spurs fans. For football, and especially a special club like Tottenham, will live on through generations, as it has done to this day. My father first visited The Lane when his uncle took him along to watch a match in the season following the 1961 double-winning season – yes, my father, a glory hunter! And my father first took me to The Lane when I was seven, a quarter of a century ago now. One day, I hope, I will take my children too, injecting Tottenham DNA into their blood. But, going to matches is just one aspect of supporting Tottenham; for supporting the club is also supporting it history, ensuring memories endure eternally, passing them down through generation to generation For although I have seen and marvelled at such footballing greats as Hoddle and Gascoigne, Ginola and Keane, it is the mental picture I have of those that I am too young to remember or see play tha inger on too. Sometimes I think their memory is almost as vivid in my head as inside that of the fans that actually saw them perform. Names such as Nicholson, Blanchflower, Mackay and Greaves are recalled with ease, somehow, like semi-religious icons whose talents are worshipped beyond their playing or managerial days, even beyond the memories of those who saw them with their own eyes. Tottenham 'til I die? No. Tottenham forever!

Anthony Trew [Photo] Bill Nicholson spreads the Tottenham message to the next generation

TOTTENHAM HOTSPUR
FOOTBALL CLUB

AND GOD WILL BE MY WITNESS

As I am well into my middle-age, I decided to make provision for my demise and therefore warned my local minister that when the time came I would like to be buried with my Tottenham scarf around me. Thinking he would be shocked, I asked him if it was an unusual request to be buried with something sporty. "On the contrary", he said, "I recently conducted a funeral for a man who requested his cricket bat be buried with him!" So, feeling that I was quite 'normal', I happened to mention to a friend of mine (who supports Liverpool, and was kindly giving me a lift home), about my wish to have my scarf with me – his reaction was to laugh so much that he nearly lost control of the wheel, at the same time, informing me that I was a 'nutter'.

The thing is I love Spurs so much that I don't want to be parted from the club after my death, it's a token of my affection for the club. I know it wouldn't help in the afterlife, however, at least I would be going over to the unknown with something familiar and precious from this life. What better thing to take on such a journey?

Because this is now so important to me I have added a handwritten codicil to my Will informing my descendants that I am to be buried with the scarf so that my wishes can be adhered to. I am so nervous that I often can't bear to watch us play – when the whistle blows for the game to commence, I can actually hear my heart pounding and develop a stomach ache. I have to force myself to look at the score during the game, and if we are losing, I pace around like a caged tiger.

Pearl Harris

Staying Brave For Tottenham

As a special treat to celebrate my eighth birthday, my dad took me to see Spurs against Arsenal, an event that would allow me to see my hero, Glenn Hoddle, and of course Tottenham Hotspur, for the first time. I knew about the outing well in advance and the excitement had been building up for months!! On the morning of the game my grandparents popped round to say hello before we left, during which time my grandad managed to shut my little finger in the sideboard leaving it hanging on by a piece of skin. My mum instinctively wrapped it in a towel and we headed for A&E as quickly as we could. By the time we got there the towel was completely wringing wet with blood. As we walked in the nurses couldn't believe that I wasn't crying or screaming out in pain, but the thing was, all

I could think of was the Spurs match and I kept telling them to hurry up. After they had stitched the finger back on and given me a drink and a lolly – off we headed up the A31 and, despite the emergency diversion, we had only missed five minutes of the match! Spurs beat the old enemy 2-0 that day, which remains one of the most memorable days of my life.

Funnily enough I lost a bit off the tip of the same finger a few years ago when a client decided to pick me up and drop me while I had a bottle of beer in my hand after a long afternoon entertaining!

Whenever anyone comments on the scar they always get to hear the story about how I was such a brave lad to avoid missing that Arsenal match.

Rich Lynn *pictured then and now*

AGAINST ALL ODDS

It was a Monday night and my mates and I had made the three-hour trip north to Hull to watch the mighty Spurs. Tottenham needed the points, as we were still too close to the relegation zone for comfort.

We had booked into a little bed and breakfast and planned on getting up there before 4pm so we had time to enjoy ourselves before the game. When we got to the stadium Steve decided to put a bet on for Tottenham predicting a 2-0 win, intrigued, and because I had never had a flutter myself, I did the same. I asked Steve to go halves with me, deciding to put a fiver on Tottenham to win 2-1 with Lennon to score the first goal at odds of 66-1. With the slip tucked safely into Steve's pocket we crossed our fingers and headed off to find our seats.

The first half started well with Lennon scoring a stunner from outside the box to give us the lead, only to see it cancelled out before the break. It didn't really sink in that Hull's equaliser was 'good' because, like all Spurs fans, we were desperate to get away from the drop zone rather than thinking about losing five quid on a bet.

The second half was fairly mixed possession-wise and it looked as if we were going to have to settle with a point. Then, in the 85th minute, a cross was whipped in and BANG! Jonathan Woodgate popped up with a header that sent the ball into the back of the Hull net. Needless to say the last five minutes was a nervy time, so bad that I had to go down and wait in the toilet because all of a sudden I was thinking about the money too much. I walked back up to my seat just as the final whistle went – a sound that left Spurs three points better off and Steve and I £330 richer. What a result, I don't have to tell you how much we were jumping around and celebrated our win, our punt had just paid for the hotel, a night out on the town and our petrol there and back. But in the celebrations, and to our complete and utter disgust, the slip had somehow got lost and, despite hunting everywhere for it under and around our seats, we found nothing! We spent the rest of that evening eating a miserable curry in the hotel room then decided simply to go to sleep.

When we got back to London the next day and had told a few people of our misfortune, I heard that there might be a way of us getting our winnings back after all, so I sped to my local bookies and asked if there was anything they could do. A helpful lady told me to fill out another slip and they would see if they could match the handwriting with the one up in Hull, the only problem with that potential solution was that, as we put the bet on inside the stadium, we would have to wait until after Hull's next match when the slips were passed on to the main bookmakers in the area. For the next few days all I could think about was the money and how gutted I was that Steve had lost the slip.

Friday came and I had received no phone call, so in desperation I drove to the bookies that evening to ask again – one last time. As I walked into the shop the same lady was there and from her mouth came the words, "I've been waiting for you to come back, if you show me some ID I can pay your bet out right now." I ran to the car to get some identification, then legged it back to be presented with a handful of crisp £20 pound notes. Wow. I immediately rang Steve and told him that I had something for him and his face was a picture when I gave him half the booty. Despite the result against Manchester United at Wembley, it was the perfect start to a Cup Final weekend!

Rob Hughes [centre] *with his mates Steve and Paul up at Hull City*

Being a Tottenham supporter for over 35 years, I have been fortunate enough to witness some memorable matches and great triumphs, especially those in the 80s and early 90s. However, the one match that really cemented my love affair with Tottenham Hotspur was not any of the usual 'classics' that are often rolled out, but probably one when we were at our lowest ebb. It was the last game of the 1976-77 season at home to Leicester City, my first proper season as a supporter, and save for some freak results going our way, Tottenham were all but relegated.

As was the norm, my uncle and I got into the ground at around two o'clock and stood in the Paxton Road right behind the goal. Despite our predicament, the atmosphere was remarkably upbeat and jovial – nobody would have guessed that we were on our way out of the First Division. I recall prior to the game, two fans went onto the pitch with a large banner proclaiming "We Will Return" to the applause of the whole ground. I don't think the Police were too bothered as the fans seemed to be able to do what amounted to a lap of honour around all four stands before being escorted off. The match itself was unremarkable, but we did win 2-0. Results did not go our way and unsurprisingly, down we were.

As soon as the game ended, what seemed like hundreds of fans invaded the pitch and chaired off some of the players as if we had just won the League! They all congregated in front of the Directors' Box in the West Stand chanting, "We all agree, Tottenham Hotspur are magic!" This 'celebration', because that's what it really seemed like, was still going on when we left the ground some 15 minutes after the final whistle. I will never forget the feeling of pride that day and it certainly helped an eight-year-old boy come to terms with the tragedy of his team being relegated.

That resolute attitude in defeat of 'so what, we're still Tottenham Hotspur and that's all that matters' still lives in me and I really couldn't care less what other teams or their fans have to say for themselves. We are Tottenham Hotspur! The likes of Gascoigne, Hoddle and Klinsmann were all great players, but my heroes will always be the likes of Pat Jennings, Terry Naylor, Steve Perryman, Chris Jones, John Duncan and Peter Taylor.

Stuart Howard *pictured on a Spurs pre-season trip to Dortmund*

Losing Nanna Bows' Scarf

Yorkshire puddings and fairy cakes. It was another wonderful weekend spent at Nanna Bows' house – a visit made extra special when she presented me with a hand-knitted Tottenham scarf and announced that my brother (14) would be escorting me (11) to The Lane for my very first live experience of the Lilywhites. And there we stood at the front of The Shelf, where he taught me how to play 'Spoof'. That was May 1971 and Huddersfield Town were humbled 4-1 with Chivers and Gilzean sharing the spoils.

Not everything went to plan that afternoon though, I remember crying my eyes out all the way home to Slough, which had nothing to do with the result. It was for fear of explaining to 'Bowsie' how my prized new scarf had somehow been ripped from my neck and disappeared at pace down the Seven Sisters Road never to be seen again.

When I told my nan that her beautiful scarf had been stolen by a fellow Spurs fan she rolled her eyes and shook her head in bewilderment, and entered into one of those 'I don't know, the youth of today!!' type conversations that folk from her era were perfectly entitled to do. She then pulled out her knitting needles to reassure me that another scarf would soon be in production and that this time she would also teach me how to tie a half-decent thief resistant knot.

Close to 40 years later and living in America the opportunities to re-visit that hallowed arena are few and far between, but I still manage to be at every game via *BBC London's* internet commentary and vicariously through my son who recently made the 7,500 mile round trip to witness the 4-0 mauling of Middlesbrough. I'm Tottenham 'til I die – I just hope I get to see the new stadium before I do!

Alan Gilbert

RISKING YOUR LIFE TO SEE TOTTENHAM WIN

My father, Arthur Bowring *[pictured left]*, is coming up to his 96th birthday and he's been a Spurs supporter all his life. His first game at The Lane was in 1921 when he was taken along by his father, Augustus Bowring.

Just after dad's 90th birthday, on April Fool's Day 2002, we were leaving White Hart Lane having just beaten Leeds in a nail-biting match – when he collapsed at the foot of the exit steps. I thought that he had fainted and a number of fans helped me lay him down on the ground inside the Paxton Road stand to await the St. John's ambulance men to arrive. They looked after him and quickly got dad in an ambulance heading off to the North Middlesex hospital. I asked my son to go with him while I went to get our car and met them there. I arrived at the hospital A&E and asked for him – they told me he was in intensive care. I was puzzled, I told them that he had only fainted, then they told me that he'd actually had a heart attack! I went into the ward and spoke to dad where he told me that he had been having pains during the game but didn't want to leave. A little while afterwards, as I got up to walk away from his bedside for a moment, dad said, "As I was lying on the concrete floor at The Lane I thought, 'This is it – but at least we won!'"

[Right] Arthur with his dad, Augustus, and mum, Emma, at Southend in 1920

He remained at the North Middlesex for the next three weeks and we visited him after each Spurs home game – he always knew whether Tottenham had won or not because, "You can hear the cheers at The Lane through the open window in the ward!"

The story ends happily because at the age of 95 dad still comes to Spurs home matches along with me (his 65-year-old son) and his grandson, who is now 21. So I guess dad really does epitomise the attitude of 'Tottenham 'til I die' – almost – but I hope he gets to see Spurs win the League again in time for his 100th birthday.

Colin Bowring

ALFIE STOKES: A CASE OF MISTAKEN IDENTITY

A. Stokes

I have to confess I was nearly an Arsenal fan! I was born in 1934 and because my brother-in-law, Frank, was on the Arsenal books as a goalie as a young kid this influenced me. Unfortunately for his footballing career the 1939-45 war intervened and he was stationed in the RAF up in Scotland. When he came home on leave he used to take me to White Hart Lane to see Arsenal play as they had to use our ground, Highbury being closed during the War and used as a civil defence centre. Because of the ground-share agreement, one week Spurs were at home, the next it would be Arsenal's turn, so we were never quite sure who we were going to watch.

When he was demobbed after the War, he used to take me to Highbury, and we were part of some massive crowds – I remember being passed over the heads of the fans down to the front, so that I could see, along with the other kids. Frank and my sister then decided to emigrate to Australia – but my move was far nearer – I decided to go back to White Hart Lane! Later on, I introduced my girlfriend to the glory of Spurs and she is now my wife of over 51 years – we are both still season ticket holders to this day. Spurs had a prolific goal-scorer in the late 1950s by the name of

Alfie Stokes, who famously once scored five goals in a 7-1 win over Birmingham City, and it was frequently said I was his spitting image.

I have to admit that I did look very similar to Alfie and kids would often mistake me for him, pestering me for autographs. On a bus going home after a match – believe it or not players used buses in those days – some boys kept asking me for my autograph, naturally I kept denying that I was a Tottenham player, but it took an older guy on the bus to help stop the kids bothering me for a signature. He sternly told the lads, "Can't you use your eyes; this man is obviously not Alfie Stokes!"

A few stops later the man got off and as he was passing, said to me, "Hope I helped you there Alfie, it must be a nuisance to keep getting pestered!"

Norman Allen *[pictured above left] or is it Alfie Stokes?*

THE REALLY EARLY BIRDS

It was December 23 1950 – Spurs were at home to Arsenal. My friend Shirley and I knew there would be a big crowd so I decided to stay at her house the night before the game. We both got up at 5.00am, had breakfast, made sandwiches, filled our flasks with hot tea and started out at 5.45am to begin queuing in Park Lane to ensure we would stand in our usual place – at the front, to the right of the Park Lane goal. Luckily a relative of Shirley's lived in Paxton Road, where we could replenish our empty flasks and use the loo if needed.

About 9.30am two newspaper photographers came down Park Lane and asked us how long we had been queuing for, when we said since around 6.00am, they asked if they could take our picture, to which we of course agreed. They asked our names and ages, and although we were only 15 I remember that we asked them if they could print that we were both 16 so we could get in to see A category films at the cinema! Just as well, as the next time we went to the Gaumont in Wood Green the manager smiled at us and said he had seen our photo *[pictured left]* in the paper.

When the turnstiles eventually opened and we were inside the ground we started to notice people were pointing at us. Then, when the regular supporters that we stood with arrived, they showed us the lunchtime editions of *The Star* and *Evening Standard* and there we were – on the front page of both papers. It then dawned on us why people kept smiling at us!

We then decided to try something cheeky; explaining to the turnstile operator about us being famous and on the front page of the papers, and would he let us jump over so that we could buy our own copies? The man on the gate said it was okay so we dashed out and back again before he changed his mind, which would have meant our long wait would have been totally in vain. We were relieved when we climbed back over and took our place behind the goal again.

And what made the day even more special was that the Spurs beat Arsenal 1-0, Eddie Baily scoring the all-important goal. My mum knew somebody who worked on *The Star* who was able to get a real copy of the photograph, which I later took to Ted Ditchburn's shop and asked him to get signed by the players.

Lorna Hall

And I'd Do It All Again

It was Boxing Day 1975, I was 22 and still living at home with my mum and dad in Orpington in Kent. I was already a regular at Spurs, going to every home game whether by train or by car with friends, although I hadn't passed my driving test. Anyway, there was a festive fixture and Spurs were playing at home to Birmingham City with an 11:15am kick-off and although my friends had decided they weren't going to the game, I was desperate not to miss the match.

Unfortunately that year, there was very little public transport running on Boxing Day – in fact there was no train or bus service from Orpington at all. So what to do? How on Earth was I going to get to the game? Obvious! Yes, walk!

I planned my route via the Rotherhithe Tunnel as it seemed to be the shortest way that was achievable on foot, somewhere between 16 and 20 miles by my estimations, but I still didn't know exactly before setting off.

I got up at some daft time and left the house at 5.00am, and what a walk! But five and a half hours later I was outside the ground. At the time I sold a few Spurs weekly draw tickets to family and friends, so I popped in to the Development Office to hand over some money. The young lady in the office wished me a Merry Christmas and told me that my friends had been looking for me

to see if I'd arrived. She said that they would meet me in the usual place in the Paxton Road stand. I told her that she must be mistaken, as my mates weren't coming.

To my horror, though, as I walked in to the ground, there they were, all standing there in front of me with huge smiles across their faces! Their story was that they had all been to a party on Christmas night and had decided to change their minds as the evening merrily wore on.

This was in an era long before mobile phones and my mum and dad didn't even have a telephone in the house. The lads said that they'd been round to my house en route, only to be told that I'd set out at 5.00am. How funny they found that! To add insult to injury, Spurs proceeded to lose the game 3-1, our only goal being a penalty from Martin Chivers.

Thank God I got a lift home after a day like I'd had, to have walked all the way back home again in the freezing cold would have killed me! We stopped in at our local on the way home, where I was the talk of the pub and my friends still tell the story to this day. And would I do it all again? Of course I would! Come on you Spurs!

David Hollingsworth *[left] at Spurs [centre] in 1976 and [Above second from left] in 2009*

The Brooks Dynasty

My dad's dad was Joseph Brooks, who had a furniture shop in Bethnal Green. He was born in 1881, a year before Spurs were formed. Both he and his dad were among the first Tottenham supporters. Grandad died in 1956, when I was young, but he used to go to Spurs with my dad, also called Joseph (born 1911), and my elder brother Gordon. They always called Spurs 'The Lilywhites'. Grandad's favourite player was Dimmock, who scored in the 1921 FA Cup Final. I like to think that people like grandad started a dynasty of true Spurs supporters and left me a great legacy of appreciating attacking, flair football. I'm very grateful to dad and grandad.

My love affair with Tottenham Hotspur started when I was a small boy – dad made sure his four children were all guided along the right path. He explained that Tottenham were an attacking, entertaining team, whereas certain other teams were not. I was born in Muswell Hill, north London in 1947 and despite dad loving the Lilywhites he just did not have the time or money to take me to matches.

Things changed when I went to secondary school and sat next to a boy who was Spurs mad. He got me to memorise the names of all the Spurs players and tested me at school. At that time, dad changed his job and his pay rose from £10 a week to over £20. Thanks to this, our lives changed significantly and I got a pocket money increase to about two shillings (10p) a week, which meant that I could go to White Hart Lane with my friend. An afternoon at Spurs cost me a shilling in total, which was two old pence each way on the bus, two pence for a programme and sixpence to get in the boys' entrance – in other words, 5p in today's money.

This being 1959, you can imagine the fabulous teams I saw play over the next few years and the honours we won, including the Double, of course. On one occasion, when I was 16, I arranged to go to Spurs with two pals and three girls, who were all supporters. On arrival, there was just one girl and myself. It was a set-up. We have now been married for 40 years.

Obviously, I brought my son and daughter up the right way too and their kids also wear their Spurs kit with pride. My daughter married a chap who happened to be a Spurs supporter. Apparently that wasn't the reason for her choice, but it helped.

Because my dad's dad was a Spurs man too, one of the first supporters, the continuation with my children and grandchildren means that we have five generations of loyal Tottenham fans in our family... and long may that continue!

Larry Brooks *pictured with several generations of Spurs fans in his family*

REMEMBERING ANDREW

Andrew was six years old, a keen footballer and wanted to support a team. The choices were Luton, Northampton, Watford, Arsenal and Spurs. It was the year of the FA Cup replay against Manchester City; the Ricky Villa goal. Andrew, lying outstretched on the carpet in front of the TV, was enthralled by "that" goal. "That's the team I want to support." Season tickets were purchased, East Stand Upper, and so began Andrew's life-long love of Spurs.

His first match was against Nottingham Forest, the first live televised League match, parachutists descending as part of the pre-match razzamatazz. For a six-year-old, this was entrancing. Spurs won and the love affair had begun. From that point on Andrew attended almost all Spurs home matches and a good many away matches. He attended the 1987 semi-final against Watford at Villa Park, which Spurs won. The Final was against Coventry; disaster, Gary Mabbutt own goal, we lost.

For 19 years, through thick and thin, Andrew was unswerving in his love of Spurs. Highlights included beating Arsenal in the 1991 semi-final, the Gazza free kick, and going on to beat

Forest in the Final. He was at Leeds for the semi-final the year we were destined to win the Cup after being re-instated; we lost to Everton. The euphoria of the League Cup win over Leicester at Wembley. The disappointment at Kaiserslautern when we lost in added time, visits to Newcastle where we always seemed to lose, the trip to Forest when the match was abandoned because of snow. Forest seem to figure prominently in Andrew's Spurs story.

And throughout this time, Andrew was growing up. Junior School, Upper School, GSCEs, A levels, University, (Nottingham, naturally), Graduate trainee with Laing Homes at various offices up and down the country, then offered a permanent position in Crawley, but wherever he was, it was home at the weekend for 'the match'. Andrew's story came to a shattering and tragic end in November 2001 when he was knocked down and killed in a hit and run incident on the Costa del Sol during a golfing weekend.

Donations were requested rather than flowers and his friends, work colleagues and family were in agreement that Andrew would want the money raised to be used for something connected with Tottenham. The Tottenham Hotspur Foundation was approached and was totally supportive, so the Andrew Duggan Memorial Cup competition was born, competed for each year by junior schools in Haringey with approximately 300 children taking part each year. The competition is in its seventh year and has become a fixture in the local schools football calendar.

Andrew would be very happy to think that his name was so closely connected with Spurs and the competition is a fitting memorial to a lifelong supporter who was truly "Tottenham 'til I die".

Jeff Duggan *pictured at White Hart Lane [back row 4th from left] in 2000*

GLORY, GLORY, HALLELUJAH

The Tottenham anthem of *Glory, Glory Hallelujah* has become a familiar part of Spurs fans' life for many years and games at White Hart Lane, but few know of its exact origins. And the answer to where and when the song first emerged may surprise many Spurs fans – January 1960 at Newport County. Spurs were drawn to play at Somerton Park in Round Three of the FA Cup that year.

In the week before the game, South Wales had endured very heavy rain, meaning that the pitch was waterlogged – by midweek the game was in doubt. Newport decided to spread loads of sand on the pitch to soak up excess rain water, so much so that *The Daily Mirror* ran a story on the Thursday in which Danny Blanchflower told fans attending the game to take a bucket and spade with them!

We set off from our Hertfordshire home very early on Saturday morning. My younger brother, Michael, wanted to come and mum advanced him some pocket-money, as he was still at school, meaning he could join our little Spurs fan club which included me, Michael, my great mate Colin Turner, Dick Skeggs and "Bubbles" Gunn. When we got home my brother told mum that it was one of his best days in his life.

And what a full day it was. A train out of Paddington, playing three card brag all the way; surrounded by hundreds of other Spurs. On the walk from the station to Somerton Park I noticed that the local Welsh shop girls stared in awe as these London boys made lots of noise and, as we approached the ground, we sang out "Bobby Smith, Bobby Smith riding through the glen" to the Robin Hood theme song. And then it happened.

Prior to the game and during the match the Tottenham fans rang out the choruses of *Glory, Glory Tottenham Hotspur*. It had started. For the record, Tottenham secured an easy 4-0 win, and after the match about 30 of us linked arms and walked side by side all the way back to the station singing our new *Glory, Glory* song. In the next round we took the song to Crewe's Gresty Road, where the lads secured a 2-2 draw on a mud heap, which saw Tommy Harmer gliding across the quagmire.

The replay at The Lane is memorable too, not least because my mate Colin was caught in traffic and,

[Pictured] *Brian and his crew in Trafalgar Square and with their flags and other fans at Birmingham New Street Station for the Cup tie against Aston Villa in '61*

[Above] Brian, in his Spurs shirt, welcomes a fellow Tottenham fan to New Zealand

[Left] Brian's brother and mates in a Wembley pub beer garden before the Cup Final in 1961

when he eventually arrived 20 minutes after kick-off, he was dismayed to discover that we were already 6-1 up. He almost fainted. The Spurs slammed in 13 goals that night. The following season, the Bill Nicholson – Danny Blanchflower style of football was really gaining momentum and as confidence grew on the terraces, our mob grew too. At the 2-0 win at Villa Park in Round Six we met up with Walthamstow girls Val Fowler, Doreen Page, Anita and Marion Milne – who was an occasional baby-sitter for the late, great John White.

Then there was the Scotsman, Jock, who worked at Mount Pleasant sorting office and his son Steve. Together we carried our infamous flag to all games, which carried the simple message "TOTTENHAM FOREVER". The last time the flag took centre stage was at the 1963 European Cup Winners Cup Final where we beat Atletico Madrid 5-1 in Rotterdam. That was the last match I saw before emigrating to New Zealand in September 1963. Despite the vast distance, being round the other side of the world has never led to my support waning and I'm proud to say that my loyal support for Tottenham will carry on forever, just as my old flag said it would!

Brian Ruck

Finding True Love At Tottenham

Andrew smiles through the tears back at White Hart Lane!

It was 19 January 2008 and my girlfriend of five years had just been caught out cheating on me. I was mortified. Three days later I was supposed to be going to the Second Leg of the semi-final against Arsenal, I just didn't want to go.

My friend talked me into it and I moped my way up from Somerset to The Lane in the passenger seat. The rest of that unforgettable night still gives me the tingles. When Lennon made it four I realised I was surrounded by exactly what I needed. Loyalty, passion, belief and hope.

There was a chap of about 40 behind me who was at the game by himself, I wondered if he had been through similar turmoil. It didn't matter a bit, when we scored the fifth he jumped and shouted, "My boys have done it! My boys have done it! Come on my boys!" I hugged that guy so hard.

On the way home I realised that every Tottenham fan I meet from now until forever will be 'my boys'. I now ensure that on every return to the Park Lane end I spare a little moment to remember that night and the positive path Spurs returned me to.

Andrew Gill

ARRESTING YOUR OWN FATHER

I was driven to becoming a Tottenham fan by my dad, who used to take me to Spurs matches, when he could afford it, during the 60s and early 70s. We lived near Colchester then so it was not always possible. When I turned 18, I looked for a job that would broaden my horizons and I joined the Metropolitan Police in 1977. My first posting as an officer, fresh out of Hendon Training School, was, to my great delight, to Tottenham Division and I was even given accommodation in Northumberland Park. In those days, police officers worked inside the ground as well as outside. My first season as a copper (1977-78) saw Spurs promoted from Division Two back to Division One. My dad used to come to games more often at that time and we would see each other in and around White Hart Lane, me in uniform, him with his blue and white scarf and woolly hat.

In March 1979, Tottenham were playing Manchester United in the FA Cup – the game was ticket only and my father had gone to the ground hoping to pick one up from a friend. When this did not materialise, he was left standing outside, ticket-less – where I was on duty.

Now I know this was wrong but, thinking quickly on my feet, I put my father's arm up his back and marched him into an entrance to White Hart Lane where arrested fans used to be kept in the ground awaiting transport to the station. I told the officer on the door I had 'nicked this guy for fighting'. Once inside, I released my 'prisoner' and he got to see the game – which ended in a 1-1 draw. Spurs may have lost the replay, but dad still delights in telling everyone about the day he was 'arrested' by his own son.

Kevin Bowsher *pictured holding a cockerel that he found while out on the beat*

Breaking Down International Barriers

The day started as a bright, warm morning. Three of us met up and drove the short distance from Walthamstow to Tottenham and parked up close to the ground. Considering it was 6.00am a lot of Spurs fans were walking to the ground and you could sense the anticipation in the air.

We arrived at the main gates and there were coaches as far as the eye could see, all the way down the High Road. At this point, as we climbed aboard our coach, Coach 13, we joked that it may be unlucky for some. Little did we know how true this would be!

We left the stadium at 6.30am in a convoy. The first hint that it was going to be a bad day was when we collided with the traffic lights at the end of the High Road at the junction with the North Circular Road. As there was no major damage to the coach, the driver carried on.

Many of the fans on our coach had 'been on it' all night and were well oiled when we left, especially the six dustmen sitting behind us. Two of them had to visit the toilet at the back of our coach 30 minutes into the journey, and as the second one reappeared from the toilet he informed us that it was blocked.

Within another ten minutes the facilities resembled medieval latrines and a river of nastiness flowed down the centre isle whenever the driver applied the breaks.

We arrived at Dover and the ferry over to Calais was fine, the Spurs army was in fine voice. We boarded our coach at Calais and were informed of severe delays en route to Belgium because of French farmer blockades, but our driver said he would take some detours to avoid them.

Spurs fans out in Anderlecht for the first leg match

We should have realised this was a bad move because 20 minutes into France, we were lost! We made our way aimlessly towards Belgium along a few 'B' roads and it was here that we came across our first blockade.

There were lorries as far as you could see – we ordered our driver to go down the side of the queue, as we were not going to miss the UEFA Cup Final for anything.

We could see that some lorry drivers had been there for hours, as they had set up tables and were eating and playing cards. We got to the front of the queue and one by one all the Spurs fans got off Coach 13 to see what the problem was. Fifteen French farmers had parked tractors across the road and no one could pass.

We walked over to explain our dilemma, but they were ready for a fight and picked up pitchforks and haysticks – then the cavalry arrived. Two more Spurs coaches pulled up and the fans poured off. We pushed all the tractors into ditches at the roadside and all the lorry drivers blew their horns in approval, we boarded our coaches again and were off. We were confronted by the same situation twice more before we arrived at the Belgium border, so we made sure that our three coach convoy stayed together.

As we arrived on the outskirts of Brussels, the rain was pouring down and at a junction a car jumped the lights as we passed through them and collided with our coach. We had to stop for a further hour until an ambulance came for the car driver and the police had confirmed with witnesses that the accident was not our fault.

We then stopped at a service station, where many Spurs fans had stopped earlier and apparently there had been an incident. The police, sensing an easy nick, boarded our coach and said unless the perpetrators were handed over everybody on our coach was going to be arrested and thrown in cells. The announcement triggered a sudden mad dash for the emergency exit door at the back

of the coach and everyone jumped off. Other coaches that were leaving opened their doors and our coach load dispersed amongst them. We arrived at the stadium 20 minutes later, and although it started raining the minute we arrived in Belgium, it could not dampen the Spurs fans.

Tottenham were superb and played a blinder. Although the match finished 1-1, Spurs deserved to win and Anderlecht only scored a fortuitous equaliser with five minutes remaining. We all left the ground happy, believing that we would easily win the second leg at home, but concerned with how we would get home.

We arrived back at the coach park and there was Coach 13 waiting at the front for us. Thankfully, the journey home was plain sailing in comparison to the journey there and Spurs finished the job off back at White Hart Lane!

Danny Grove

THE STORY OF THE FLYING PIG

"C'mon!" shouted mum, "We're going to the match!"
"Okay!" I replied. I rushed down the stairs, tumbling over as I went. Yes! For once my mum was going to take me to see my favourite footy team play against Manchester United. I've played for Spurs' youth teams since I was four years old and am still being coached by them; I'll play for Spurs anytime, anywhere.

The drive to White Hart Lane whizzed by, all of a sudden we were outside the home stadium of the best team in the world. Oh no! Some bloke was blocking the road to the car park. "Hey mate," I called out to him... "I've got some news for you..." "What is it?" he replied. "YOU'RE BLOCKING MY WAY INTO SPURS!" I exclaimed. After what seemed like an hour, and with the help of the police, the man finally came off the road allowing us to park our car and head off to the ground to find our seats.

"Ooooh, ahhhahh," the crowd exclaimed as they marvelled at a pig flying around the stadium. The people forgot about the flying pig and focused on the match as it began. "It's Robbie Keane with

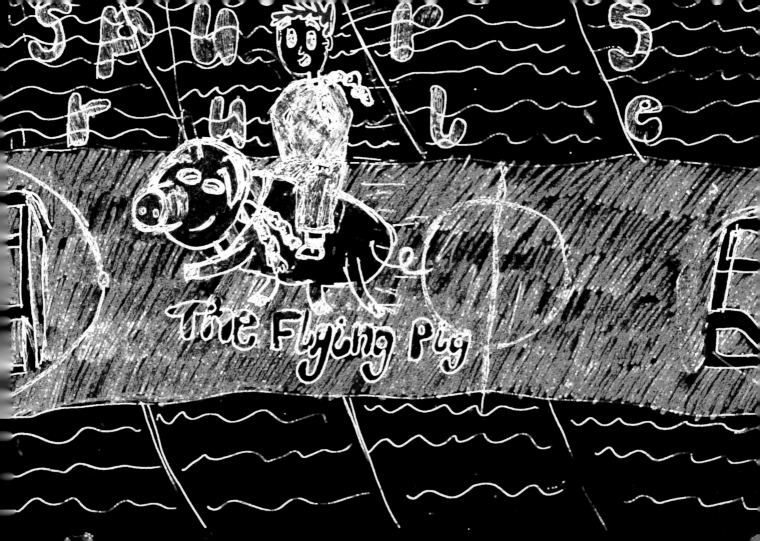

The Flying Pig

the ball," the commentator said after 20 minutes of the game. "He's beaten two defenders, he shoots, he scoooorrress, oh no!" At just that moment the flying pig had swooped down and saved the brilliant strike.

Then minutes later, Aaron Lennon had another go at goal, but again, the pig pulled off a stunning save. At this time people in the crowd started going out on to the pitch and joining in with the match. Soon there was nobody left in their seats, including me.

At 89 minutes the score was 10-10. David Bentley and Robbie Keane had scored some great goals and so had some of the fans. But somebody needed to grab a winner for Tottenham, but who would it be? Suddenly I received a pass, and I knew what I had to do with the ball. Off I set, taking on everyone on the entire pitch.

"And it's a lad from Saint John Fisher Catholic Primary School on the ball," I heard the commentator say. "He's coming up to the keeper, he shoots, he scores! It's 11-10"

"YESSS!" I shout, punching the air. Then the final whistle blew. Thank God we had won!

Chinedum Mgbatogu *pictured on previous page* [**above**] *children from Saint John Fisher reading out their Spurs stories*

I LOVE MY TOTTENHAM

My name is Carly and, although I'm only seven years old, Tottenham are my favourite thing in the whole world. From the moment I could talk I've sung all the songs; *Glory Glory Tottenham Hotspur* being my favourite.

I fell in love when my mum and dad walked me down to White Hart Lane when Spurs were playing Arsenal. We didn't have tickets but mum wanted me to feel the atmosphere. I loved it and was singing all the way home.

My teacher supports Arsenal so I tease him a lot, and I tell him that my homework will have to wait if 'my' Tottenham are playing!

The best time ever was when we won the Carling Cup again and we walked to The Lane after the game. The whole of Tottenham was full of Spurs fans, it felt like every one of them was my best friend and we all danced and sang together.

Before every match I cross my fingers, but no matter what the score is, I love my Tottenham!

Carly Coldwell *from Churchfield School*

Whiskey In The Bottle

I have seen some of Tottenham greats play like Arthur Rowe, Bill Nicholson, Willie Hall, George Hunt and Cecil Poynton, who we always affectionately called Ginger, and a number of others whose names I have unfortunately forgotten over time.

During the 1930s, there were two principal goalkeepers, Cyril Spiers, who played somewhat like Gomes has in recent times, making some great saves and then letting an easy one go in. The other goalie was Joe Nicholls, he was a giant. He would come onto the pitch, walk to the goal, and with both feet firmly on the ground grasp the crossbar with both hands.

At that time there was an outside-left named Willie Evans, he was no Aaron Lennon, but he had a terrific left foot. He would kick the ball first time with such force that the first thing one saw was a great hump in the net and the ball bouncing inside the goal. On one occasion he cracked a goal post with a shot, on another, Joe Nicholls anticipated the arrival of the ball and attempted a save, which broke his hand.

During a match over the Christmas period in the mid 1930s, Spurs were awarded a free kick just inside the opponents' half, near the touch line where I was standing. Taffy O'Callaghan, a popular player at that time, came to take the kick. A spectator near me offered Taffy a miniature bottle of whiskey, which Taffy took and put in a pocket in his shorts – he took the free kick and scored!

I watched Spurs for a number of years until as a youth I played in a minor league (Stoke Newington & District) where I won a silver medal when we finished runners up. I was offered a trial for Tufnell Park, then the Arsenal nursery, but I did not want to be a professional footballer.

I was a member of St.John Ambulance Brigade before and after WW2 and, in July 1939, I was conscripted into the Royal Army Medical Corps and served with the BEF in France, Eighth Army in Egypt and Normandy, then on to Germany. I left the army in 1946.

Walter Hart

[Left] Walter with his father in 1931
[Above] Walter during World War Two
[Above Right] Willie Hall and the players greet new signing Andy Duncan in 1935

Nothing Could Get Past Me

My Degree was taken at Birmingham University within the College of Food, Tourism and Leisure Management – now I am working as a football coach as part of the disabilities team within the Tottenham Hotspur Foundation. Although the situation has improved in recent years I must admit that when I was writing my study there were some grounds which were very difficult for disabled fans to get into and once inside, the facilities were also very variable. At a well-established London Premiership club I once attended a Cup game where I had to watch the second half of the game on the little televisions because the people in front were standing up and we could not see any of the play. Unfortunately this was after I had finished my dissertation.

My work takes me into the three local Boroughs of Haringey, Enfield and Barnet where historically our support is strongest. One of the achievements I am most proud of was when I played power chair football at National League level. And only a few years ago I went to Japan to learn more about the large ball variant of the sport. Another memorable moment, was being voted disabilities coach of the year for Barnet. One of the best things about teaching through football is the way that it helps people to overcome negative attitudes. In the early 1990s I attended a well known special school and even there I came across negative attitudes regarding disabled people playing football such as a fellow student asking, "How can you ever hope to play football when you're in a wheelchair?" Many years later I proved him wrong.

I like to think that I have personally proved that anyone can do what they really want to do if they give the time and commitment. One of the greatest pleasures for a football coach is to witness the progression over the weeks, with players starting from virtually nothing and gradually picking up the different skills. Seeing youngsters playing and knowing that I am part of helping them to experience such feelings is the real reward for the work I and the other coaches do. The hard part is the long hours. Sometimes I work until nine o'clock in the evening. In addition to working in schools and within the Tottenham Hotspur Foundation, I also coach with Whetstone Wanderers, which is quite a large club. The attitude of the other coaches at Whetstone has been nothing short of fantastic in the way they have received me into the club. Thankfully, they have accepted me as one of their coaches and taken the mickey out of me on a consistent basis. This may sound a small thing but so many organisations have the wrong attitude towards disabled people. They either ignore them completely or are completely over-the-top in the way they communicate with you by treating that person as 'special'. I have also travelled as a coach as far as Swindon and Newcastle with teams representing Tottenham Hotspur.

I'm sometimes asked what the best game of my playing career was, and I have to say it was when we played against Aston Villa. I had the game of my life. Nothing could get past me. I was the Pat Jennings of our team, stopping everything. Yet in contrast, when I was playing in Japan, I was taken off by the manager half way through. At the time, naturally I was upset, but to be honest my performance that day was poor; or as some would say, I had a shocker, a Freddie Kruger of a game!!

As a Spurs fan there have been many memorable moments both good and bad. We all remember being three goals up against ten-man Manchester City only to concede four and lose. And then there was that game against the other team from Manchester in September 2001 when we went three goals up through Richards, Ferdinand and Ziege only to concede five in the second half.

Can you imagine my luck? I'm involved in something that I love most; football coaching, and also working for the Club's Foundation that is part of me.

Danny Jarvis *pictured with Pascal Chimbonda*

Dedications

Alan Tomlinson
Adam Conn
Emma Conn
Alex Conn
Adrian Pomfrett
Alan Gilbert
Aled Major
Paul Smith
Elliott Taliesin Alter
Moss Costas Boys
Brett R. Nurse
Andy Aarons
Andrew Boorman
Andrew Bryce
Andy Gray
Andy Minton
Andy Tuckwell
Ann Bonner
David Hill
Warren Boon
Anthony Taylor (ROLLY T)

Arun Debnath
Mark Wells
Austin Mclaughlin
Paul Grant
Sam Shaw
Barry Camfield
Joshua Willcox
Barry Cantello
Patrick Hicks
Barry Rose
Ben Parkinson
Alec Parkinson
Glenn Wells
Andrea Williams
Brian M Standord
Brian Ruck
Robert Horstead
Catherine Jackson
Lewis Williamson
Cheryl Muggeridge
Chris Burn

Chris (Boggy) Burrows
Paul (Snowy) Snow
Andrew Snow
Chris Cullinane
Chris Hennebry
Chris Levin
Chris James
Nicholas Dowdeswell
Chris Mantz
Christopher Peacock
Christopher Zavros
Stephen Snowball
Colin Glennon
Colin Kendell
Oliver Phillips
Colin (Tom) Pearse
Glen Pearse
Craig Grant
Craig Hubbard
Craig I Humphries
Jamie Damhuis

Craig Lowrie
Dave King
Dag-Erik Bjerknes
Damon Osborne
Damon Pearson
Dan Mackenzie
Daniel Borgersen
Daniel Christopher Clark
Daniel J Fisher
Daniel Hartley
Danny Lesar
Sarah Louise Pikarski
Daniel Ripley
Ellie Louse Hart
Darren Curran
Lorcan Fitzgerald
Kealan Fitzgerald
Tiernan Fitzgerald
Darrin Percy
Luke Jol Pitman
Dave Bosher

Dave Spackman	Dean Smith	Daniel Trainor	Billy Murrell
David Atkinson	Dean Tomlinson	Gavin Mcguire	Jamie Thorogood
David Beecham	Dean Wells	Matthew Brown	Alexander Constantine Sarantis
David Cramphorn	Deborah Rye	Emma Brown	Jan Johansson
Dave Eagles	Ronald Knight	Geoffrey K Raven	Janis Carter
David Harris	Denise Knight	Charlie Douglass	Jarrod Hayes
David Horne	Katherine church	Houtevels Gert	Jason Dawson
David Jordan	Derek Barry	Giles Stacey	Jason Pauk Evans
Steven Langridge	Tony Ireton	Giuseppe Mastroianni	Paul Spencer
David Mitchell	Donna Bolitho	Glenn Hutton	Jean Cusker
Tom Mitchell	Duncan Morris	Gwyneth Carty	Rhian Fudge
Paul Mitchell	The Brand Boys	Curtis Osbourne	Jeffrey Kaye
David Paveley	Eliot Solarz	Mrs H Tufton	Ian Robert Toop
David Pile	Tim Edwards	Heather Shaw	Gavin Rice
David Price	Martin Davis	Hidell Ross	Eoin Rice
David Relf	Enrico Di Filippo	Ian Bonner	Gareth Foynes
Alan Relf	Erik Sorensen	Ian Bonner	Mark Rawlins
David Scannell	Fiona Ives	Ian Dearman	Matthew Hodgetts
David Stannard	Alan Clarke	Ian Murphy	Craig Collins
David Taylor	Gareth Posnett	Ivan Elliot	Joe Bacon
David Thomas	Gary Allen	Brian Fitzpatrick	Joe Chubb
Dave Wiseman	Gary Davis	Jacquelyn Pick	Joe Regan-Page
David Wood	Gary Evans	James Evans	Joel Sapiro
Mark Armitage	Gary Griffiths	Michael Moore	John Crockett
Peter Greenaway	Gary Sumsion	James Pearce	John Deer
Lee Taylor	Gary Thirkettle	Matt Norris	John Fennelly

John McCarthy	Norman Trew	Mark Lever	Michael Mcgough
Jon Laugharne	Kieth Ward	Mark Salvin	Paul Mcgough
Jonas Byford	Lennart Pettersson	Terry Salvin	Michael Stapleton
Jonathan Edwards	Stephen Boddy	Mark 'Skippy' Skinner	Michael T Cleary
Jonathan Salmon	Leslie Boddy	Mark Urso-Cale	Michelle Dolan
Joseph Christal	Michael Boddy	Mark Wallbridge	Michelle Hastie
Justin Crump	Lewis Baker	Mark Wheeler	Michelle Webb
Justin Rockberger	Lewis Buckler	Martin Avis	Mikael Blomberg
Keith Tuley	Lorraine Innes	Martin Brown	Mindaugas Ambraska
Richard Berndes	Kevin Dodkins	Luke Crabb	Myrianthos Demetriou
Tony Sims	Alan Dodkins	Martin Dharwarkar	Myrna Hughes
Karl Holmes	Mick Brierley	Martin Helt	Nasser AlQadi
Paul Everson	Pops Bannon	Jasmine Milcoy	Nathan Ramsay
Philip Pinder	Marc Gulikers	Martin Kennedy	Neil Buckley
Keith Durkin	Frank Mendel	Martin Taylor	Neil Gilbert
Keith Lowe	Marc Oxby	Darryl Taylor	Neill Walsh
Keith Preston	Marcus Goddard	Matthew Coulson	Nick Weston
Jennifer Ryan	Marcus Macdougall	Matthew O'Gorman	Nicholas M Tribley
Dylan 'Bannerboy' Rushton	Marek Markowicz	Meng Howe Tan	Nicholas Rees
Neil Taylor	Ricky Clay	Michael Armstrong	Nick Hughes
Ken Kenyon	Mark Bond	Michael Banbury	Nick Sutton
Kenn Pedersen	Mark David Carnwath	Daniel Banker	Daniel Edwards
Kenneth Andre Dimmen	David John Carnwath	Michael Bankover	Bugs Bicknell
Ken Odgers	Mark Fairhall	Michael Bennett	Nigel Bicknell
Kevin Claxton	Mark Fissenden	Michael J Hammerton	Nigel Jeny
Peter Dunham	Mark Jackson	Michae Jordan	Nigel Holmes
Kevin Edwards	Judy Lloyd	Michael Langan	Noel Purcell

Norvald Soleng
Oliver Hardwick
Tricia Boak
Patrick Roberts
Paul George
Popeye
Paul Kennedy
Paul Kottaun
Paul Richards
Paul Sainty
Paul Shea (Shaggyy)
The Sutterby Family
Paul J Villeneuve
Paul Wakeling
Peter Addyman
Peter Corfield
Peter Riley
Peter Sampson
Peter Swanson
Peter Unsworth
Petter Melbye
Pew Kan
Phil James
Philip Todd
Jack Bonney
Ole Norman
Rebecca Brooks

Richard Barlow
Sarah Atkins
Richard Gunstone
Richard Levene
Richard Mandy
Richard Rochester
Richard Ryan
Rick Mayston
Ricky Burke
Julia Dick
Robert K-Petterson
Rob Moore
Robert Tremblett
Rod Nolan
Ronnie Baird
Russell Pereira
Ruth Brooks
Ryan Scott
Daniel McDermott
Christopher Scott
Sarah Selby
Scott Doyle
Scott Haynes
Scott Jenkin
Sean Edwards
Sean Hanratty
Sergios Latis

Mark John Hills
Darren Ashley
Sam Ruff
Shaun O'Dea
Sidney Faulkner
Simon Burton
Sjur Flage
Steve Pettican
Dean Pettican
Stephen Savory
Stephen Wakeling
Alan F Burkett
Steven Burkett
Steve Keen
Steve King
Andy king
Steven Abrahams
Steven Butt
Steven Smyth
Stuart Roy Baker
Keely Franklin
Kier Franklin
Earl Franklin
Shelby Franklin
Shaw Franklin
Joe Bliss
Keith Franklin

Mark W Ford
Barry Strows
Suzanne Draycott
Sverker Otterstrom
Tahir Masud
Thomas McMichael
Thomas Newey
Thomas Towers
Thor Kjell Kaddeberg
Andreas Kaddeberg
Tony Fearon
Trond "Trondski" Legreid
Veronica Woodhatch
Roger L. Woodhatch
Roger T. Woodhatch
John Woodhatch
Stephen Woodhatch
Terry Lockwood
Walter Hart
Stella Sipple
Wesley Livingstone
William Osborne
Max Rogers

The Spurs fans named above have supported the production of this book by taking part in the advanced purchase scheme.

'Til I Die

This book enables fans to come together to share and write stories about their club. *Tottenham 'Til I Die* is one of eight new books which tell the stories of local football fans; all of them by fans, for fans. These books are a roll-out from the immensely successful *Brentford 'Til I Die*, a Football League community award finalist in 2007. The project is a partnership between the *National Literacy Trust* and *Legends Publishing*; funding is from the *Department for Children, Schools and Families* and the *Football Foundation*. *Tottenham Hotspur Foundation* also contributed. Some of the proceeds from the sales of this book will provide free books for local schoolchildren, which will help to encourage local children to love reading as well as football, and so increase their opportunities to succeed in life.

Jim Sells *Manager, Reading The Game*
National Literacy Trust

National Literacy Trust

LEGENDS PUBLISHING

FootballFoundation
football's biggest supporter

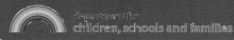
department for children, schools and families

Contributors

This book was developed, designed and produced by David Lane and Steve Cowan at Legends Publishing. A very big thank you to Anna Rimington, Julia Brosnan and the staff at the Tottenham Hotspur Foundation for their help and enthusiasm. Other contributors include:

Daniel Levy	Phil Brackstone	Danny Grove
Darren Shan	Alan Gifford	Danny Jarvis
Justin Hynd	Sue Franklin	Walter Hart
Emad Nimah	Keith Palmer	Irfan Master
Dylan Rushton	John Niblett	
Martin Brown	Geoff Niblett	
Lal Hardy	Sonya Lipczynska	
Mark Kersey	Dave Jordan	
Chris Stevens	Myrna Hughes	
Dave King	Anthony Trew	
Harvey Harris	Pearl Harris	
Gary Raynor	Rich Lynn	
Sid & Harry Tobias	Rob Hughes	
David Brooks	Stuart Howard	
Anna Gillespie	Alan Gilbert	
Ken Nighingale	Colin Bowring	
Chinedum Mgbatogu	Norman Allen	
Carly Coldwell	Lorna Hall	
Nick Weston	David Hollingsworth	
Alan Fitter	Larry Brooks	
Graham Bishop	Jeff Duggan	
Gareth Dace	Brian Ruck	
Michelle Dolan	Andrew Gill	
Larry Cotton	Keith Bowsher	

Thanks to everyone who contributed to this project, unfortunately we simply did not have the space to reproduce every story that we were sent.

It's not too late to contribute your Spurs story, visit *www.tilidie. co.uk* **and send us your tales. The** *'Til I Die* **website also includes fans stories from an ever-growing list of football clubs.**

WWW.TILIDIE.CO.UK